Flight Lessons 2: Advanced Flight

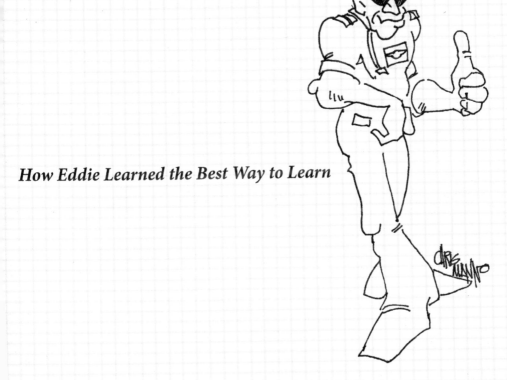

How Eddie Learned the Best Way to Learn

James Albright

Acknowledgments

Thanks to Chris Manno for over thirty years of trading aviation stories, writing techniques, and for permitting my blatant grand larceny of his artwork without complaint. Thanks also to Chris Parker for all the fact checking, sense of grammar, and style pointers. If he's told me once, he's told me a thousand times to avoid hyperbole.

James' Lawyer Advises:

Always remember that James, when you get right down to it, is just a pilot. He tries to give you the facts from the source materials but maybe he got it wrong, maybe he is out of date. Sure, he warns you when he is giving you his personal techniques, but you should always follow your primary guidance (Aircraft manuals, government regulations, etc.) before listening to James.

Contents

The Notes Continue

Eddie's Notebook

After a year of Air Force pilot training (flying the T-37B Tweet and the T-38A Talon), and after two years flying the KC-135A from the frozen forests of Northern Maine, I had accumulated hundreds of pages of notes but there was still much more to come. My notebook included everything from basic instrument flying, to jet formation flying, to dealing with engine failures. So that is where we have come from and you can find all that in Volume One: Basic Flight. I learned very quickly that a pilot's *attitude* toward learning determined his or her *altitude* as an aviator. A pretty good deal for a young pilot at the ripe age of 25. But I was ready for more.

This next book in this saga finds us in Hawaii with the Boeing 707 (EC-135J) and then Nebraska with the Boeing 747 (E-4B). I arrived at both squadrons at the peak of their influence, filled with very good pilots and very good missions. The problem with being the new guy in a squadron of excellent pilots, is that few of those pilots are interested in passing on their knowledge and skills. It was left up to me to find the best way to learn when there was no teaching going on. So there you have it, Volume 2: Advanced Flight.

Each chapter contains a story of the flight lesson as I learned it, followed by the flight lesson as it exists today, on graph paper. The stories are as I would have written them at the time and the flight lessons are from today's perspective, with all the knowledge that has been gained since. The graph paper pages include references to sources in [brackets] which are given in the back on page 214. Where my personal techniques and opinions are given on these pages, they are shown in blue.

Oh yes, the names. All of the names, even my own, have been changed.

A word about security clearances is in order. Most of us know that there is a security clearance called "SECRET" and another called "TOP SECRET." But few know there are clearances above and below that. Below "SECRET" you have "CONFIDENTIAL" and above that the names of the clearances themselves are classified.

In the second portion of this book we delve into the world above TOP SECRET. The unclassified name for this is known as Sensitive Compartmented Information, or SCI. Each security classification resides in its own compartment and the name of the compartment itself is considered classified. At least that is the way it is supposed to work. You can actually type "Sensitive Compartmented Information" into your Internet search engine and come up with a bunch of them.

The information is so sensitive, they constantly spied on us to make sure we adhered to these clearances. I once underwent surgery while in an SCI program and a special agent had to remain in the operating room at all times in case I started talking while asleep. (I didn't.)

As an Air Force officer entrusted with SCI information, we were required to keep tight lips on such things and when leaving a program that required the clearance, we were debriefed and told to never again utter another word about it.

So I've left out everything that can possibly be inferred as part of the compartments I was involved with. Instead, I made up a compartment that I called PATRIOT BLUE. I've never heard of such a compartment but the nature of these things is if you aren't briefed into them, you will never know. So just to be clear: PATRIOT BLUE is fictitious. (At least I think it is.) Well then, now we can begin.

1: Secrets

Hickam Air Force Base, Honolulu, Hawaii
1982

EC-135J From Boom Pod of a KC-135A (Haskel Photo)

The secrets began on day one. "It is the tan building behind the airplanes," he said on the phone. "Park in the lot just mauka, come to the gate and ask for me. There are no signs."

"Okay," I said, "see you." He assumed I knew mauka meant toward the mountains.

I knew my sponsor was Hawaiian from his name, Captain K. Walter Keku-mano. That's about all I knew. Since the 9th Airborne Command Post had a secret mission, few on base knew it even existed. The four Boeing 707s, designated EC-135Js, were pretty silver and white birds with nothing to give away their mission except the words "United States Air Force" along the length of the fuselage. From the unmarked parking lot I could see the four tails towering over the bunker that I assumed would be my home for the next several years. The building was surrounded by barbed wire and the solitary front gate was guarded by a sentry with a rifle. In the periphery I saw two more guards in standard issue blue trucks.

As I approached the gate, I noticed a single sign notifying me that the use of deadly force was authorized. As the guard studied my orders and picked up a phone, I looked beyond the fence to the building. Two dark brown doors, one of which had the familiar 9ACCS squadron patch, set off the light brown exterior. The nearest door suddenly opened and a tall, dark haired captain strolled out, smiling. He waved at me and shot the guard a thumbs up. The gate opened and I entered, saluting the captain. "Good morning, sir."

"Call me Walt," he said, returning my salute. "It will be nice to have another local pilot here," he said.

"How many we got?" I asked.

"Including you and me?" he asked.

"Yes, sir."

"Two," he said. "And don't call me sir. You can call the majors and lieutenant colonels sir, but you and me are the same. We copilots got to stick together."

We entered the squadron just as two majors were leaving. The shorter major looked me in the eye briefly and then back to the other major. "Christ," I heard him say, "a damned lieutenant."

"Don't let him bother you," Walt said. "That's Greco. He hates everyone." I got the nickel tour as we gathered all my in-processing paperwork, my new flight manuals and flying regulations, and a new set of flight suit patches. The scheduling office had the standard grease pencil board probably found in every Air Force squadron, this one with five crews on top and unassigned extras on the bottom. That's exactly where my name was. I had a flight scheduled in a week.

"You get as many rides as you need," the scheduler said. "Then you get a check ride. But don't take too many. The more rides you take, the meaner Greco gets."

"Ten rides is the record," Walt said. "Most guys get good enough to hang on to the tanker by five or six. Don't worry about Greco. He has a rough exterior but he hardly ever busts anybody." I scanned the board and noticed three empty slots for copilots. I knew from experience that when a squadron is short copilots, training gets rushed and check rides get easier.

A week later I was approaching the new airplane for the first time with my instructor pilot, Major Bobby Duff. He wore senior pilot wings and wanted to talk about sports, politics, or anything other than the EC-135J. "It is just another airplane, Eddie. Don't worry about it."

After two years of flying a gray tanker with tiny little engines and an empty cargo bay, the new bird was like eye candy for a pilot. The EC is white and silver, has massive engines, and is covered from nose to tail with strange and wonderful antennas. The interior is filled with communications equipment, passenger seating, and two things I had never had before on an airplane: a flush toilet and a galley. It was all a treat, but nothing caught my eyes more than the engines.

"Are they reliable?" I asked Major Duff as we approached.

"Haven't lost one yet," he said. "Lots of thrust at your command at a moment's notice."

I lowered myself into the right seat, opened the checklist, and started flipping switches. Once or twice I came upon something I'd never heard of before and Major Duff would point to the new gizmo and I would move on. Duff spent most of his time chatting with the navigator or giving an endless editorial about the state of the Air Force promotion system. His monologue continued into the flight.

He flew the airplane almost as an afterthought. He manipulated the controls and glanced outside now and then, but he spent most of his time with a running commentary about what our navigator was doing during the rendezvous with the tanker. Once he spotted the tanker, he moved on to a play-by-play of the tanker's maneuver. Our airplane was flying a very smooth line from a mile back and a thousand feet below, around 310 knots. In a few minutes we were fifty feet behind the tanker and at 275 knots. My only duties were to open the fuel receptacle doors and the three or four valves needed to escort the fuel from the tanker to our wing tanks. I stole a few glances of the throttles and Major Duff's hands to decode the secret of getting an airplane flying at over 400 knots true airspeed to within 50 feet of another airplane safely. It remained an act of magic.

"Stabilized, pre-contact, ready," Major Duff said on frequency. The boom operator acknowledged and we slowly advanced toward the tanker. As the boom traced a line over our heads, I could hear a whoosh until the clunk of metal-to-metal contact.

"Pumping gas," the boom operator said. I looked down to see our fuel panel lights acknowledge the fact.

"See how easy this is, Eddie?" Major Duff pointed to a UHF antenna on the bottom of the tanker with a white line painted just forward. "Just make the antenna and the line an upside-down T and you can't go wrong."

But how do I do that? The tanker would attempt to fly straight and level and provide a stable platform. But flying our 300,000 lb. airplane precisely behind and below at 25,000 feet was hardly child's play. Ailerons, rudders, and elevators have less air to bite in the thin air and I could feel the airplane wander in each axis. I could see more than a few ways to go wrong; it was as if he told me the perfect golf shot was hitting the ball 300 yards off a tee into a small cup in the ground. Easy. And I had a check ride to face.

He explained that all a copilot had to be able to do was take control of the aircraft in case the pilot was incapacitated and move the airplane aft in a controlled manner. "So I'm going to give you the airplane and we'll see how long you can hang on. Ready? You got the airplane."

I tried to keep my control inputs as small as possible, but in just a few seconds we were moving right. "Left ten," the boom operator commanded. I dipped the left aileron just a little and soon I heard, "right ten." There seemed to be a time delay built into each control surface, with the magnitude and duration of the delay determined by a Las Vegas bookie. I was unable to predict the outcome of each input. The oscillations only got worse and before we knew it I heard the boomer announce, "disconnect." I was startled by the boom flying over our heads and jerked the throttles back. In just a second we were a half-mile in trail. I added an inch of throttle and felt the nose of the airplane jerk up. "Geez!" I heard from the navigator.

"These engines are very responsive," I said. I started to formulate another wry comment to explain my inept performance, but was interrupted by the unmistakable sound of the navigator losing his lunch.

Major Duff laughed. "Believe it or not," he said, "this isn't awful for your first try."

"Speak for yourself," the navigator said.

"Maybe if you add a little rudder things will smooth out for you," Duff said. I did that but things just got worse. Once we ran out of tanker time we headed for Kona Airport, on the Big Island of Hawaii. I was prepared for the airplane to have even more Dutch roll than the tanker and was not disappointed. The EC-135J has bigger engines, slightly larger wings, and essentially the same flight controls. Both aircraft were designed before aeronautical engineers really understood Dutch roll on a swept wing jet and the Air Force never bothered installing electronic fixes. Both aircraft required active pilot inputs to stay right side up. But I was a pro with Dutch roll.

"Very nice," Duff said as I lined up on the 6,000-foot runway jutting out from an ancient lava flow. At 50 feet I brought the throttles to idle and felt the aircraft sink. "I got it," Duff said. He shoved the throttles forward and we climbed back to pattern altitude. "Let me show you one." As he brought the airplane back around, I tried to analyze what had happened. When I brought the throttles back, the lift disappeared. It didn't make sense.

"We are almost 50,000 pounds heavier than that tanker you used to fly," he said. "You can't chop the power. As we descended through 50 feet, he pointed to the throttles. "Watch this." He pulled them very slowly and they never really got to idle until the wheels touched. "See? See? You try it."

That worked for some reason I didn't understand; every approach and landing after that was just fine. My training record was 90 percent praise for instrument approaches and landings, but under the column for receiver air-refueling he entered only two words: "needs work."

I rushed home to my engineering texts and aircraft manuals in search of an answer to the mysterious new engines. I had never worked a day in my life as an engineer, but an engineering degree left me thinking of myself as an engineer first, pilot second. I understood why the airplane pitched up with added power behind the tanker almost as soon as it happened. The engines are below the wings and adding thrust to all four would pitch the nose up. But I hardly added more than an inch of throttle. That kind of power change wasn't unusual in the traffic pattern and the nose never popped up on me then.

The EC-135J's engines produced 16,050 pounds of thrust of which about half, just looking at the diagrams, appeared to come from the fan of the engine that completely bypassed the core of the engine. The KC-135A's engine produced just over 9,000 pounds of thrust, all of which came from the engine's core. None of that engine's air was bypassed.

Two of my textbooks verified what I had learned that day: higher thrust engines with larger bypass ratios carry more of their power at the top end of throttle travel. Closer to idle the engines put out much less as a proportion of their maximum values. While the EC-135J had more thrust, it was also heavier and the ratio of thrust to weight decreased at lower throttle lever angles. An inch of throttle at low power settings changed thrust by a little. An inch at higher power settings, at 25,000 feet behind a tanker for example, changed thrust a lot.

I looked at my notes with a satisfaction only an engineer could appreciate, knowing I had solved my throttle and pitch issues. But that smugness came to an end when I realized I still didn't have an answer to my air refueling mystery: how do you keep the airplane centered behind the tanker plus or minus 8 degrees?

The next day I was introduced to the rest of the copilot force, including a name from my past, Kevin Davies. We shared instructors during pilot training as second lieutenants. As an Air Force academy graduate, he had almost a year of seniority on me. "Captain?" I asked.

"Pinned on last week," he explained. "Just a copilot, just like you."

"So what's the key to air-refueling?" I asked.

"It is a secret," he said. "If I told you I would have to kill you."

"It seems that way," I said. "Any time I asked Major Duff a question his answer was always 'you'll get it, Eddie.' I'm not sure I'm getting anything."

"The thing about being in a small squadron like this," Kevin said, "one with a one-of-a-kind airplane, is that nobody really instructs. The old heads know what they're doing and can't be bothered to teach. You just have to watch and learn."

"What's the deal with Major Greco?" I asked.

"Greco sucks," he said. "He got me on my first check. I busted the oral."

"Oral?" I asked.

"He picks a topic you are guaranteed to know nothing about," Kevin said. "He just wants to hear you say something wrong so he can prove he's smarter than you."

"I've never been offered a practice oral," I said. "I wonder if I can get an instructor to do that for me."

"Don't bother," Kevin said. "You only get an oral on your initial check and nobody but you cares."

Training sortie two was with instructor pilot Major Don Wortham. "Keep your feet off the rudders," he said as I corrected from five degrees left of the tanker. "Those things can kill you at this altitude." Like Major Duff, Wortham flew with a nonchalance that disguised any real effort, never deviating from the center of the air-refueling envelope. He let me fly it even when the boom operator's voice raised an octave or two. I managed to hang on to the boom for a good sixty seconds before falling off.

"That's going to do fine," Major Wortham said. "You are ready for a check."

"What?" For the first time since pilot training, I felt completely unprepared for an assigned task. With three years as an Air Force pilot I had become accustomed to grasping concepts sooner rather than later and eventually flying every maneuver just as the textbook demanded. But there was no receiver air-refueling textbook and measuring my abilities against the pilots I had flown with only pointed to my shortcomings. Now I was up against a major that hates lieutenants and has his own standards. My official pilot record book included fifteen check rides, all of them either "Exceptional" or simply "Qualified." But none of them were failures. Yet.

Principles of Propulsion

Figure: Principles of propulsion, from [Hurt, figure 2.5]

[ATCM 51-3, Pg. 105] You can summarize how a jet engine works with two of Newton's Laws of Motion. Newton's second law can be written as:

$$F = ma$$

A force F acting on a mass will cause the mass to accelerate in the direction of the force. The mass is air passing through the jet engine.

Newton's third law of motion states that for every action force there is an equal and opposite reaction force. The action force is the air mixture accelerating aft, the reaction force is on the engine itself, accelerating forward.

But what does that really mean? The mass being accelerated aft is fuel and air mixture. The mass is pushing against various components of the engine which in turn push the engine (and therefore the airplane) forward. On some aircraft, like the early KC-135A, water is added to the fuel air mixture to increase the mass being accelerated.

Figure: Centrifugal compressor, from [Hurt, figure 2.7]

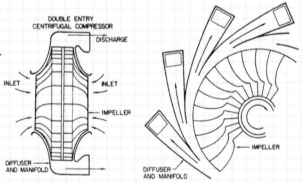

[Hurt, pg. 109] The compressor must furnish the combustion chamber with large quantities of high pressure air in a most efficient manner. Since the compressor of a jet engine has no direct cooling, the compression process takes place with a minimum of heat loss of the compressed air.

The centrifugal flow compressor has great utility, simplicity, and flexibility of operation. The operation of the centrifugal compressor requires relatively low inlet velocities and a plenum chamber or expansion space must be provided for the inlet. The single stage centrifugal compressor is capable of producing pressure ratios of about three or four with reasonable efficiency.

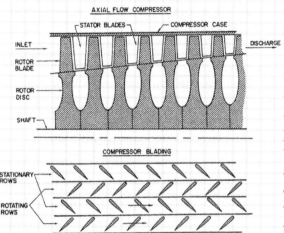

Figure: Axial compressor, from [Hurt, figure 2.7]

[Hurt, pg. 111] The axial flow compressor consists of alternate rows of rotating and stationary airfoils. A pressure rise occurs through the row of rotating blades since the airfoils cause a decrease in velocity relative to the blades. Additional pressure rise takes place through the row of stationary blades since these airfoils cause a decrease in the absolute velocity of the flow. While the pressure rise per stage of the axial compressor is relatively low, the efficiency is very high and high pressure ratios can be obtained efficiently by successive axial stages. The multistage axial flow compressor is capable of providing pressure from five to ten (or greater) with efficiencies which cannot be approached with a multistage centrifugal compressor.

Figure: Combustion chamber, from [Hurt, figure 2.8]

[Hurt, pg. 111]

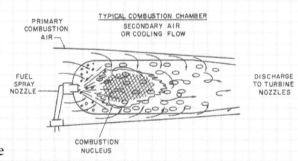

The combustion chamber must convert the fuel chemical energy into heat energy and cause a large increase in the total energy of the engine airflow. The combustion chamber will operate with one principal limitation: the discharge from the combustion chamber must be at temperatures which can be tolerated by the turbine section.

The combustion chamber receives the high pressure discharge from the compressor and introduces approximately one half of this air into the immediate area of the fuel spray.

The fuel nozzle must provide a finely atomized, evenly distributed spray of fuel through a wide range of flow rates.

The temperatures in the combustion chamber nucleus can exceed 1,700° to

17

1,800°C but the secondary air will dilute the gas and reduce the temperature to some value which can be tolerated in the turbine section.

The typical introductory text might lead you to believe this is where thrust comes from: the gas explodes aft, pushing the combustion chamber forward. But most burner cans are hardly the robust structures that can withstand this amount of force. There is something else in play here . . .

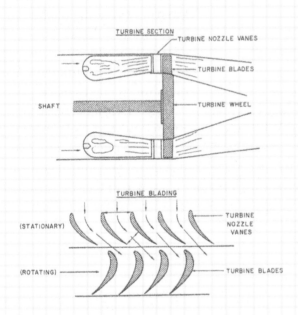

Figure: Turbine section, from [Hurt, figure 2.8]

[Hurt, pg. 113] The turbine section is the most critical element of the turbojet engine. The function of the turbine is to extract energy from the combustion gases and furnish power to drive the compressor and accessories. In the case of a turboprop engine, the turbine section must extract a very large portion of the exhaust gas energy to drive the propeller in addition to the compressor and accessories.

The turbine nozzle vanes are a row of stationary blades immediately ahead of the rotating turbine. These blades form the nozzles which discharge the combustion gases as high velocity jets onto the rotating turbine. In this manner, the high pressure energy is converted into kinetic energy and a pressure and temperature drop takes place. The function of the turbine blades operating in these jets is to develop a tangential force along the turbine wheel thus extracting mechanical energy from the combustion of gases.

The rotating turbine blades are where all the heat and pressure are converted into the mechanical energy used to rotate the forward fan (or propeller), run the accessories, and most importantly to push the center shaft forward. This is where thrust gets transmitted to the airplane and this is another reason the bearings holding that shaft in place are so critical.

2: Grasshopper

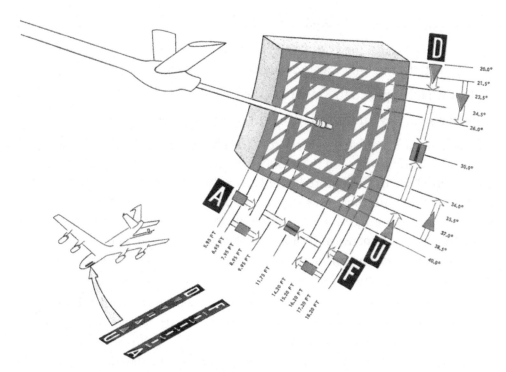

Receiver director lights (1C-135(K)A-1, figure 4-54)

Crew One was the standardization and evaluation crew, the guys who gave everyone else their check rides. They had the senior pilot, copilot, navigator, and so on down to members of the communications team. Working your way down from Crew One to Crew Five, you had younger crewmembers in each position. Crew One was the top of the food chain and my introduction to the new squadron would forever be characterized by what Major Dan Greco thought of my skills on the next sortie.

"Greco sucks," I saw on the squadron bathroom wall. I had flown an orientation flight with him and made face-to-face contact a few times. But every glance I ever got from him was an unmistakable sneer.

"He's rough around the edges," Walt said. "He starts out mean and ornery, and then he gets downright spiteful and vindictive."

"Really?"

"No," Walt laughed. "Major Greco is a stickler for doing things the safest way possible, but he has a narrow definition of what that is. Just don't get on his bad side. Once you are down the Greco pit of spite, there's no digging

19

yourself out."

"What about the oral?" I asked.

"It's a rite of passage," he said. "You can't prepare for it and you can expect to be humiliated. The only way to really fail it is to start arguing with him."

"Is that what happened to Kevin?" I asked.

"Yup," he said. "Whatever you do, don't lose your cool."

I showed up at his office the day before the check ride, just a few minutes early. The secretary invited me to sit while she announced my presence. She gestured me in and before I could salute he asked me to sit. He had a weathered face with the crow's feet that betrayed years of smoking that had suddenly become unfashionable in the officer corps. He couldn't have been more than 5 foot 5 inches and might have pushed the scales at 120 pounds, but just barely. As a major not yet up for lieutenant colonel he could not have been older than 40. He looked 50.

"I got one rule that must be obeyed, lieutenant." He spoke from behind his desk, but sat upright and aimed his gun sights directly at me. "We are all in the process of learning, so mistakes are inevitable. But you must always respect the limitations of the airplane and keep it inside the operating envelope. We don't have a formal cornering speed, but if it were up to me, it would be the first thing on the first page of our flight manuals. Got that?"

"Stay in the envelope," I said.

"Damned right," he said. "So let's meet up tomorrow at 0600 and get this done. Dismissed."

I left his office with thoughts of flight envelopes and cornering speeds and realized my aeronautical engineering knowledge had atrophied over the years. Making the turn into the hallway I felt a large hand grasp my shoulder for the start of an unmanly bear hug.

"Two rides and a check, Eddie?" It was Walt. "You are going to do great. Did the baby killer have anything to say to you?"

"Major Greco wants me stay in the envelope and think about cornering speed." I said. "Cornering speed? Really?"

"Don't worry about that," Walt said. "Greco is a history major who fancies himself a fighter pilot. He talks that way all the time and everyone humors him."

Humor aside, I realized I needed to get smarter on the EC-135J's operating envelope. I camped out at home with my favorite aerodynamic textbooks, trying to learn what Greco knew about our operating envelope that I didn't.

The operating envelope for any aircraft can be found on its V-g diagram, so called because it plots airspeed (V) against load factor (g). The left side indicates the airplane's stall speed and the right its "red line" speed. Positive and negative g-limits border the top and bottom. If you stay in those borders at all times you should have a long and prosperous career. The V-g diagram changes with weight, altitude, and configuration; so most manuals should have a diagram for various conditions. I flipped through my EC-135 manual looking for the V-g diagram for heavy weights at air-refueling altitude.

There were no V-g diagrams for any conditions at all. How can I know my operating envelope if it isn't published? We used to do these in school, how hard can it be? I had charts for stall speeds at all conditions and the top speed was 350 knots. The book clearly said we had up to 2.0 positive g's and no lower than 0 g's, so no negative g's at all.

I dived into my college textbooks and relearned the process of building V-g diagrams. With a clean sheet of graph paper and colored pens, I created an EC-135 V-g diagram for a maximum weight aircraft at air-refueling altitude.

At first, it looked rather ordinary. The maneuvering speed looked high, but it is, by definition, the 1-g stall speed times the square root of the positive

EC-135C V-g Diagram (300,000 lbs, clean configuration, 25,000 feet)

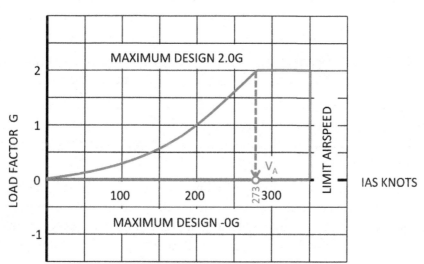

g-limit. I supposed 273 knots made sense for a 300,000 lb. airplane at 25,000 feet. With another sheet of paper I found maneuvering speed for a 250,000 lb. airplane was 248 knots and for a 200,000 lb. airplane was 221 knots.

What the military texts called cornering speed the civilian texts called maneuvering speed. So how does cornering speed come into play with a four-engine behemoth trailing a tanker at 25,000 feet and 275 knots? My V-g charts showed our air-refueling speed was just about at cornering speed at maximum weight, but much lower as our weight decreased. We risked stalling as we got slower or if we subjected the airplane to g forces. Those g forces could result from turbulence or a novice copilot getting too aggressive with pitch. I was wiser, but I wasn't sure this knowledge was going to make air-refueling any easier.

The next day, Major Greco was in perfect form, he had the steely-eyed evaluator routine down to a science, never betraying the slightest positive encouragement. From the minute we approached the airplane to the moment he brought us 50 feet behind the tanker, he had said nothing that wasn't specified by the flight manual. The only thing out of the ordinary was the unfiltered Camel cigarette perched between his lips.

"Not yet," he said after I lifted my plastic-covered checklist, my finger parked on the one item left to accomplish. He took his right hand off the throttles, pulled the smoke from his mouth and snuffed it in an ashtray to his left. "Now." I opened the receptacle doors.

"Stabilized, pre-contact, ready," he said on the radio. With an imperceptible push of the four throttles, we inched forward and made contact. Greco flew the airplane around the next turn and once we rolled out said, "you got it."

The airplane was in perfect trim, and for nearly a minute I didn't move anything. "Thirty, twelve, center," the boom operator said, "very nice."

"Thank you," I answered. The thirty degrees of elevation had been a hard one for me to get in previous flights, but Greco's elevator trim made it easy. With the pitch ironed out, the extension of the boom became easy too. Our envelope was from 6 feet to 18 feet, with 12 feet being optimal.

As several thousands of pounds of fuel moved from the tanker's fuel tanks into ours, the tanker would have a tendency to speed up unless they smoothly reduced power. We would be getting heavier, of course. As we started to move aft I nudged the throttles forward, almost imperceptibly, and got ready to compensate with pitch pressure.

"Five left," the boom operator said. I was spending so much time with my eyes glued to the tanker's fuselage and my concentration focused on the thrust versus pitch equation, I forgot to keep my eyes moving. Scan the wings too, I reminded myself. "Five right." I felt a drop of sweat running down my cheek. The azimuth limit was a good 10 degrees left and right but I had been a frequent visitor to 12 during my training sorties.

"Smaller inputs," Greco said.

"Approaching turn," our navigator said. The tanker's left wing dipped and I tried to follow suit. After half the turn we shot off to the right. It was my best performance yet.

"Good enough," Greco said, "we can send them home."

The tanker departed back to Oahu and we set our sights on the island of Kauai. After a four-engine ILS to a missed approach, a three-engine VOR approach to a missed approach, and then a visual approach to a touch and go landing Greco seemed satisfied. He flew us back to Honolulu and we retreated to his office. All that remained was an oral exam on a topic of his choice.

"Tell me how and why this airplane flies differently than the KC-135," he asked, lighting another Camel.

"I've been looking at that from an aerodynamics point of view," I said. "Now that I've had three flights in the airplane, I've been thinking about how the theory matches with my brief experiences."

"You haven't been flying the airplane for a long time," Greco said. "I get that. Now answer the damned question."

"Yes, sir." I said. "The operating envelope is narrower in the EC and that makes sense. The g-limits are the same but at any given weight, the EC stalls at a higher speed. When you add the fact that we are almost 50,000 pounds heavier before you add the first drop of fuel or first passenger, you are going to end up with a smaller envelope."

"That's exactly right," Greco said, taking the bait. He talked at length about the reasons for our smaller operating envelope, going into detail about our increased parasite drag due to the extra antennas and additional yaw problems with an engine out. While I didn't know half the stuff he was talking about, all I had to do was nod my head as if I did. The easiest orals, I knew, were the ones where the examiner did most the talking. "It's a damned shame," he continued, "that we don't have a good V-g diagram in the book."

"I drew up three for you, sir," I said, interrupting. Greco sat silently as I laid the three charts down in front of him. "All three are at 25,000 feet, one at 200,000 pounds, one at 250,000 pounds, and the third at 300,000 pounds."

"So cornering speed is right here," he said, pointing at the intersection of the positive g-limit and the stall line on the maximum weight chart.

"Yes, sir," I said.

"What is the stall speed at maximum weight and 25,000 feet?" he asked.

"The book says 193," I said. "That's a pretty comfortable margin when you are air refueling at 275."

"Unless you are pulling g's," he said. Of course he was right. Pulling any kind of g load gets you to the stall sooner. He rifled through each chart and settled back on the maximum weight example.

"With any kind of turbulence or pilot-induced oscillation," he said while pointing to the chart, "stall speed shoots right up. Eddie, this is fantastic. We can finally explain why it is so important to keep pitch oscillations to a minimum."

"I hadn't thought of that, sir," I said. "What I was thinking was the closer to the stall we are, the higher the angle of attack and the more thrust that is required. And more thrust makes the possibility of pitch oscillations even higher."

"Exactly right!" he said. Major Greco made me go through the mechanics of constructing V-g diagrams and in the end thanked me for the charts, the aero lesson, and for doing so well on my check ride. He never verbalized how well and I never found out until the next week.

"Exceptional!" Lieutenant Colonel Johansson said as I entered his office after he called my name. "Eddie, I think that's a first. Dan is pretty hard to please but somehow you figured it out. Well done!"

I was a bit embarrassed by the grade. It certainly wasn't an exceptional performance, but I guess the oral had to count for something. The grade wasn't broadcast to the rest of the squadron and I decided it was best kept a secret. The squadron assigned me to Crew Five, led by Captain Nicholas Davenport. He was the only aircraft commander in the squadron who wasn't a major and the only one who looked like a lifelong member of the Air Force weight control program.

"Call me 'The Nick,'" he said at our first meeting. "That's what everyone calls me."

The Nick led me into the scheduling office where a grease pencil board revealed the pattern to our top-secret missions. The squadron always had an airplane with a team of Navy passengers somewhere in the Far East. That left the rest of the squadron back in Hawaii for training. Crew Three was in Korea, so our crew had two weeks to go.

A week later we were at 24,000 feet, 310 knots, heading beak-to-beak with a tanker in the opposite direction at 25,000 feet.

"There are three secrets to receiver air-refueling," *The Nick* announced after handing over aircraft control, "you master these and you'll never have problems behind the tanker."

"What are these secrets," I asked while nudging the throttles forward.

"Do you expect to grasp the pebble from my palm on your first try?" he asked. "Knowledge must be earned, grasshopper."

Minimize pitch movement, I reminded myself over and over again. The square root of 2, I told myself. Make every change of power slight and counter those with elevator to minimize changes to pitch. It worked; I managed to hook up with the tanker on my first try and held on. "Not bad," *The Nick* said.

"Small power changes," I said to myself, "and wait."

"Secret One is no longer secret," *The Nick* said, "and at such a young age!"

I chased the tanker around the first turn, pressing the inside rudder. "Whoa," *The Nick* said, "not so much rudder." I backed off. "You ever heard of V-A?"

"Maneuvering speed," I said as I fell behind in the envelope. Nick took the airplane and got us close again.

"You got it," he said. "What is maneuvering speed?"

"For an airplane with no negative G tolerance, it is the stall speed times the square root of the positive acceleration limit."

"No," he said, "not the formula, the definition."

"It is the speed at which the airplane will neither stall or over-stress in pitch."

"And what happens if you introduce rudder?" he asked.

"I don't know," I said.

"I don't know either," he said. "So let's treat the rudder with care."

As I thought about that, things started to settle down and I realized I was subconsciously matching the tanker's wings to my own. The turn had become easy. "The tanker's wings become my horizon," I said to myself over the interphone.

"So, grasshopper, you have learned the first and second secrets on day one." *The Nick* gave me a thumbs up from the left seat. "A quick study," he said turning in his seat to face the navigator, "we must keep an eye on this Asian." The nav said something without using the interphone. It couldn't have been as complimentary. *The Nick* was not persuaded.

"Good job, copilot-san."

A week later *The Nick* was holding our airplane rock steady behind a tanker, almost perfectly. Our elevation was 30 degrees and our extension was 12 feet but he was about five degrees right of center. He stayed there for ten minutes.

"If you can plant this thing five right," I asked, "why not plant it dead center?"

"Good question, grasshopper." Of course he wasn't volunteering the answer. After a minute he started throwing hints. "Put your hands on the yoke and tell me if something, anything, appears odd to that brain underneath your yellow skin."

I did as requested. My first thought was there was little movement, perhaps a tremble. "Top notch 'less is more' with the controls," I said.

"No," he said, "that ain't it."

I looked down at the yoke for clues my hands would not give me. "The yoke," I said in astonishment, "is a good deal right, asking for a right bank."

"Are we banked to the right, grasshopper?"

"No."

"What causes lift?"

"A differential in pressure," I said from years of aeronautical engineering, "between the top and bottom of the wing."

"And what happens to the pressure on the top of the wing when flying just below and behind the tanker?"

"It increases of course," I said, "which robs the receiver of lift and requires more thrust."

"What if a receiver with a wide wingspan, oh, like us, is offset to one side or another? Wouldn't that make the change in lift different on each wing?"

"It would make the wing on the outside," I said, thinking aloud, "our right wing right now, produce more lift and that would induce a roll to the inside. So to counter that…"

I looked again at the yoke. It was now obvious.

The Nick moved the airplane to the left, now five degrees left. The yoke was tilted heavily to the left and yet we were wings level to the tanker and to the earth. "Now watch me move back to the right, but notice what I do with the ailerons."

The Nick relaxed the yoke's tilt to the left but then put most of it right back in. He repeated that, over and over, but the return position of the yoke was getting progressively smaller until it was zero. And dead center is where we sat.

"Moving right," I said, "you move the ailerons right but you keep them biased to the left. The neutral position to the left is to the left."

"Secret number three," *The Nick* said, "is revealed."

"Mango five one," *The Nick* said over the radio, "request disconnect." The tanker fired the disconnect circuit. The boom nozzle released itself from our receptacle and we crept backwards fifty feet. "Now you try it," he said.

And so I did, rock steady in the center of the envelope. "Sneak to the right a little." I did. "Now back to center, slowly." I did that too. "Teach more," *The Nick* said to the rest of the crew over the interphone, "I cannot. Knows what he needs to know, this Asian does."

I flew the next two turns parked in the middle of the air-refueling envelope wondering why these secrets were not revealed on day one. Perhaps the entire training program could have been written into a manual. *The Nick* was obviously a good instructor but it was a game to him. The other instructors were excellent demo pilots, but they were not in the business of teaching. It was a pity. As the new guy, I was in the business of learning.

V-g Diagrams, Theory

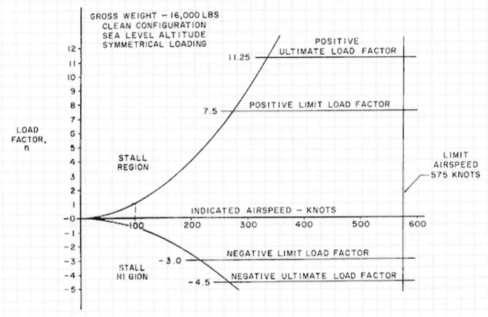

Load factor in many classic texts is labeled "n" but has become "g" in keeping with pilot phraseology.

Figure: Flight strength diagram, from [ATCM 51-3, figure 5.3.]

[ATCM 51-3, pg. 334] The operating flight strength limitations of an airplane are presented in the form of a V-n or V-g diagram. This chart is usually included in the aircraft flight handbook in the section dealing with operating limitations. The V-n diagram presented [in the figure] is intended to present the most important general features of such a diagram and does not necessarily represent the characteristics of any particular airplane. Each airplane type has its own particular V-n diagram with specific V's and n's.

The flight operating strength of an airplane is presented on a graph whose horizontal scale is airspeed (V) and vertical scale is load factor (n). The presentation of the airplane strength is contingent on four factors being known: (1) the aircraft gross weight, (2) the configuration of the aircraft (clean, external stores, flaps, and landing gear position, etc.), (3) symmetry of loading (since a rolling pullout at high speed can reduce the structural limits to approximately two-thirds of the symmetrical load limits), and (4) the applicable altitude. A change in any one of these four factors can cause important changes to operating limits.

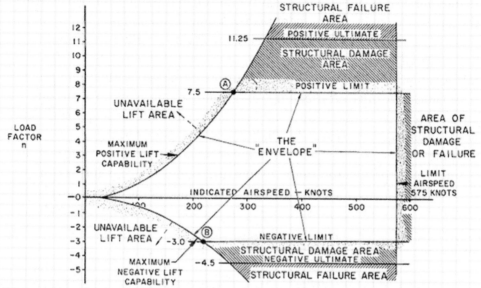

Figure: Significance of the V-n diagram, from [ATCM 51-3, figure 5.4]

[ATCM 51-3, pg. 334]

The [second figure] provides supplementary information to illustrate the significance of the V-n diagram [shown earlier]. The lines of maximum lift capability are the first points of importance on the V-n diagram. The subject aircraft is capable of developing no more than one positive "g" at 100 knots, the wing level stall speed of the airplane. Since the maximum load factor varies with the square of the airspeed, the maximum positive lift capability of this airplane is 4 g at 200 knots, 9 g at 300 knots, 16 g at 400 knots, etc. Any load factor above this line is unavailable aerodynamically, i.e., the subject airplane cannot fly above the line of maximum lift capability.

The limit airspeed (or redline speed) is a design reference point of the airplane — the subject airplane is limited to 575 knots.

The airplane must be operated within this "envelope" to prevent structural damage and ensure that the anticipated service life of the airplane is obtained. The pilot must appreciate the V-n diagram as describing the allowable combination of airspeeds and load factors for safe operation.

There are two points of great importance on the V-n diagram of [the second figure]. Point B is the intersection of the negative limit load factor and line of maximum negative lift capability. Any airspeed greater than point B provides a negative lift capability sufficient to damage the airplane; any airspeed less than point B does not provide negative lift capability sufficient to damage the airplane from excessive flight loads. Point A is the intersection of the positive limit load factor and the line of maximum positive lift capability. The airspeed at this point is the minimum airspeed at which the limit load factor can be developed aerodynamically. Any airspeed greater than point A provides a positive lift capability sufficient to damage the airplane; any airspeed less than point A does not provide positive lift capability sufficient to cause damage from excessive flight loads. The usual term given to speed at point A is the "maneuver speed," since consideration of subsonic aerodynamics would predict minimum usable turn radius to occur at this condition. The maneuver speed is a valuable reference point since an airplane operating below this point cannot produce a damaging positive flight load. Any combination of maneuver and gust cannot create damage due to excess airload when the airplane is below the maneuver speed.

When I learned this in 1979 there was a well known caveat that was articulated this way: "Maneuver speed protection is not available for a rolling pull up." In other words, if you combine roll with pull, all bets are off. After the crash of American Airlines 587 in 2001, it has been articulated in another, more useful way: Maneuvering speed is valid only when considering pitching moments with no aileron or rudder input. The old schoolhouse wisdom that "you cannot stall or overstress an airplane at V_A" is wrong. The formula for V_A deals only with pitch and stall speed; and it varies with g (you can stall an airplane above V_A if you increase the load factor.

The maneuver speed can be computed from the following equation:

$$V_P = V_S \sqrt{n \text{ limit}}$$

where

V_P = maneuver speed

V_S = stall speed

n limit = limit load factor

Of course, the stall speed and limit load factor must be appropriate for the airplane gross weight.

It is vitally important to realize this number is valid only for the computed gross weight, altitude, and configuration.

3: Technique

Two EC-135Js over Diamond Head (USAF Photo)

The scheduling board in any flying squadron gives you the vital signs you need to measure the organization's pulse, blood pressure, and respiration. Our squadron's scheduling board revealed a subtle hypertension with hidden causes. The crews were busy and turnover was high. Where crews were missing people, crewmembers from other crews had to pick up the slack. Everyone had a case of a mystery 7-Day absence that rotated from Crew One to Crew Two to Crew Three, and so on. In a week Crew Five would be in the rotation without our navigator who was on the mainland visiting family. Each member of our crew had the week blocked off for "Westpac" as did the navigator from Crew One. I stared at the entries, thinking how to best translate the codes without appearing too stupid in front of the scheduling staff.

"Westpac," I heard from behind me. "You know what that is, Eddie?"

It was Captain David White, our guest navigator for the week to come. "West Pacific trip," I said, "though that really doesn't tell me much."

"It's all in the vault," David said, "follow me and we can get this done in a day." I followed him to the navigator's office and watched as he twirled the black knob on the cabinet, stopping carefully at the four or five numbers on the round dial required to unlock the top drawer. In a few seconds he had a two-inch thick satchel labeled "TOP SECRET" and a grease pencil cover sheet with our crew's number and the trip dates. He handed me four flight plans and I went to work adding fuel computations to his navigation log. We were headed for Clark Air Base in the Philippines, Osan Air Base in Korea, and Yokota Air Base in Japan. David's navigation log was filled out neatly and I tried to duplicate his flawless penmanship. Before too long *The Nick* dropped by, reviewed everything, signed his name to the top sheet of paper, and got up to leave.

"We need to talk about anything?" I asked.

"Nah," he said, "you look like you know what you're doing." He resumed his way to the door and stopped. "You do know you can't tell anyone where we're going until that day's flight plan is filed, right?"

"Big rocks into little rocks," I said. Satisfied, he left. I had heard the phrase more than once when getting my security clearance upgraded from SECRET to TOP SECRET. The punishment for getting it wrong started at Fort Leavenworth with hard labor and worked its way up to death.

The following Monday, as *The Nick* handed our completed flight plan to the air traffic control specialist at base operations, our destination was officially declassified. It was to be a day of firsts: my first flight as a crewmember to Japan, my first flight with a load of Navy brass passengers, my first flight with a flight attendant, and most notably, my first flight with a radio operator.

"You do crossword puzzles?" *The Nick* asked once we had reached 36,000 feet with the autopilot doing the work of staying on altitude and the navigator doing the work of staying on course.

"Sure," I said. I think I had done two or three in my lifetime.

"Well get started," he said, handing me a stack. "Last one finished buys the first round tonight."

"I'm going to be busy with position reports," I said.

"We don't do no stinking position reports, boy-san." *The Nick* pointed aft where our radio operator was huddled over the navigator's table, getting his instructions. "We got people to do that for us."

Nine hours later the flight attendant came forward with hot towels. *The Nick* took two and sat back with his face covered for a minute. With a flick of a wrist both towels were on the tray left on the cockpit center console and *The Nick* announced it was time to start down. It seemed a bit early to me but I kept silent. The descent worked out perfectly.

Two days later we were heading north to Korea and it was my turn to impress the crew. As we neared the Korean peninsula, *The Nick*, normally easy going, was visibly squirming in his seat. He kept looking at the navigation log and the inertial navigation system at his side. I set mine to the distance remaining setting and waited for 115 miles. "Let's start down," I said.

"Okay," *The Nick* said. He got our clearance and I pulled all four throttles until the engine pressure ratio gauges read 1.35. I felt my ears pop. "Whoa," *The Nick* said, pushing the inboard throttles forward. "You need more power to keep the pressurization up."

"The book says 1.5 EPR minus 0.15 per 5,000 feet below 40,000," I said.

"The book is wrong," he said. "Besides, you should have started down much earlier. We're going to need half our boards." With that he disabled the inboard spoilers and pulled the speed brake handle. There were three sets of panels on top of each wing designed to spoil lift but they were designed to work as a unit. Disabling the panels closest to the fuselage would minimize the disruption of the airflow over the tail. I was technically the pilot flying the airplane, but now I was doing so with some added supervision.

"How did you know we needed to start down earlier?" I asked. "And I don't remember a procedure that allows the speed brakes to be split. In the tanker we started down at three times the altitude in thousands plus ten," I said.

"Is this a tanker?"

"Well, no."

"Try it my way, grasshopper." Of course it worked.

My notebook of EC-135J techniques was growing into its second volume and I started to catalog where each trick had come from. *The Nick* was racking up a chapter to himself but his explanations were usually, "you just figure these things out, grasshopper."

When asked about when to start the descent, what the book calls a "Top of Descent," *The Nick* only said, "I start down after the flight attendant gives me my hot towels." After a week I figured he was usually using around four times his altitude in thousands. When we got home I pulled out my book of trigonometry tables and realized that came to a 2-1/2° descent, versus the 3° most airplanes used. It made sense that we needed a shallower descent, as our fuselage was peppered with extra antennas and all those holes had to do a number on our cabin leak rate. But why did 3 times the altitude make 3° when 4 times the altitude made 2-1/2°? I needed to get back into the math.

It wasn't simple division at all; it was trigonometry with a co-incidence of math. I felt I had discovered aviation's equivalent to the Theory of Relativity and soon realized that not only

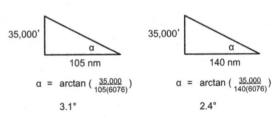

$$\alpha = \arctan\left(\frac{35,000}{105(6076)}\right)$$
3.1°

$$\alpha = \arctan\left(\frac{35,000}{140(6076)}\right)$$
2.4°

did four times the altitude in thousands worked for the EC-135J, it worked for a reason. I proudly showed my work to Kevin Davies who produced a handwritten table of his own. "One of the pilots gave me a list of altitudes and distances that seem to work," he said. "I also got a list of which pilots say always split the speed brakes, which say never split the speed brakes, and the ones that have rules that go both ways."

I scanned his page of pilot techniques and realized some were 180-degrees out from others. "This is nuts. The standardization pilot says do it one way, the training pilot another, and the squadron commander preaches his own technique."

"Yeah, it is worse than nuts," Kevin said. "Some of the pilots will yell at you for being an idiot and Greco will bust you on a check ride. And none of this is in any of the books."

"I thought procedures were mandatory and techniques were optional," I said.

"You thought wrong," Kevin said. "That second page took me almost a year to figure out. You owe me, Eddie." My thoughts were opposite his. Some-body owed me for withholding this information.

"Shouldn't we be doing it the way the squadron commander wants it?" I asked. "Johansson's the ranking officer and he is in charge, after all."

"Johansson's gone," Kevin said. "He just put in his papers. Mark Christ jumped too; he's headed for American Airlines. At this rate, I'll be running the squadron in a few weeks."

Descent Math

For those days you are told to start down "at your discretion," give the FMS a vote, but you make the final decision. There are two good start down points depending on your airplane and your arrival expectations, 3 or 2.5 degrees.

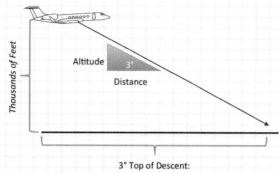

3° Top of Descent:
Distance to Start Down = Altitude (in thousands) x 3

Air Traffic Control used to be designed around the idea most airplanes are most efficient flying a three degree descent and there are still parts of the world where you can do this. Figuring it is easy. The rule for descents is that your gradient equals flight levels divided by nautical miles to go. If you use a 3.33 degree descent, the math becomes easy . . .

We can hardly detect 0.33 degrees so we'll just call it 3:

Start descent at three times your altitude (in thousands of feet) to achieve a 3 degree descent.

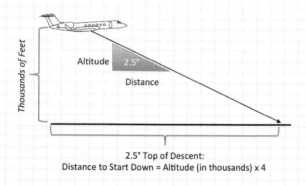

2.5° Top of Descent:
Distance to Start Down = Altitude (in thousands) x 4

Not all aircraft can manage a 3 degree descent. The G450, for example, cannot do 3 degrees at high altitudes without picking up speed. It can, however, manage half a degree less. The math for a 2.5 degree descent is just as easy for 3.0 . . .

The actual math comes to 2.4°, which is close enough to 2.5°.

Start descent at four times your altitude (in thousands of feet) to achieve a 2.5 degree descent.

If you are at 45,000 feet, for example, round the altitude up to 50, just to make things easy, and start down at 4 x 50, or 200 miles out.

If you are descending to a high altitude airport, you may want to adjust for the field's elevation. If our previous example was for a desent into an airport with an elevation of 5,000 feet, the math becomes 4 x (45-5), or 160 miles out.

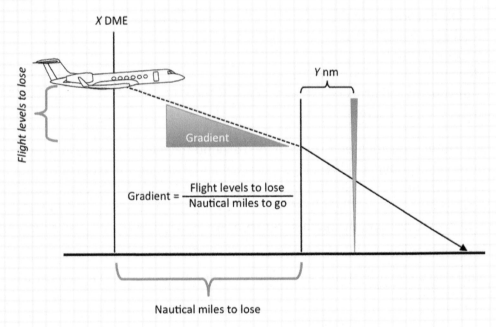

$$\text{Gradient} = \frac{\text{Flight levels to lose}}{\text{Nautical miles to go}}$$

What happens if you don't have a choice and are told to get down within a fixed distance? You could program that into your FMS and chances are it will make it happen. But sometimes it doesn't. You should always come up with your own answer to check the FMS or to have a Plan B for the days the FMS throws up its hands and says, "I don't know, you do it."

You can compute a required descent gradient by dividing the flight levels to lose by the nautical miles to go.

Required descent gradient = flight levels to lose divided by nautical miles to go.

For example, if you are at FL450, heading directly for the ABL VOR and when passing 150 DME are directed to descend to and maintain FL250 at 100 DME, you will need a (450 - 250) / (150 - 100) = 4 degree descent gradient.

4: Lieutenant Tutti Frutti

9th ACCS (USAF Photo)

In the space of a month we got a new commander, three new copilots, and two new navigators. Crew Five, for the first time in a year, was looking senior. "Pity," I said to *The Nick*, "I was hoping for a new nav."

"Better the devil you know," *The Nick* said. "Besides, Lee isn't the worst." That was high praise for Major Lee Vandunk, a navigator prone to busting check rides and getting lost in the middle of an air-refueling rendezvous. As a major he outranked us both, but as a navigator he answered to us both in the pecking order. It obviously grated on him; every request from the front two seats hit him like an unreasonable imposition on his time.

"Hey I think we overshot the orbit," *The Nick* said on our next training sortie. "The tanker's radar return is almost in front of us."

"Huh?" Vandunk said. "Well actually, that's his beacon not his return."

"But either way . . ."

"Yeah," Vandunk finally said. "Okay, turn right fifteen."

We finally joined up and I settled in for my turn behind the tanker. *The Nick* hummed quietly as I held the airplane steady to allow the boom operator to plug us. In the corner of my eye I saw the refueling status lights on the glareshield move from "Ready" to "Contact" and heard the unmistakable sound of fuel rushing into the plumbing just aft of the cockpit. The tanker dipped its left wing and I matched its bank with my right hand on the yoke and left on the throttles. I moved my head to use the tanker's wing as a visor against the impending glare as we turned into the sun. Behind me I heard a bang followed by a shout.

"Fire!"

"Break away, break away, break away!"

I pulled all four throttles to idle and held the pitch firm, preventing the nose from falling, which would have caused us to accelerate in front of the tanker. "Positive separation," I heard from the boom operator. I looked left to see *The Nick* wearing his oxygen mask.

"Your turn," he said, "I've got the airplane." I donned my mask as *The Nick* took inventory.

"What have we got?"

"Comm team reported fire forward."

"What do you see, nav?"

"Well actually," the navigator began but failed to finish.

"What do you think, Eddie?"

I keyed the mike on the air traffic control frequency. "Mango five one declaring an emergency, fire in the cabin, we need an immediate return to Honolulu."

"Okay then," *The Nick* said. I'll get us on the ground. Go back and take a look."

The Nick flew our normal descent schedule while I took off my mask and unstrapped. From nose to tail there was no sign of fire, only a sweet, pungent smell. The communications team looked terrified, the crew chiefs looked amused, the passengers looked perturbed, and the flight attendant sat with her eyes closed, almost in a fetal position in her seat.

"No evidence of fire," I reported, "only an electrical smell."

Thirty minutes later we were on the ground. The fire department scoured the airplane and found the culprit. It was a pint container of Tutti Frutti Kool-

Aid powder. The flight attendant admitted that when the sun entered the cockpit windows during our turn she was startled and dropped the container and a metal carafe. The powder turned into a cloud that an electrical rack fan threw into the air. The communications team all pointed to the youngest member of their group for yelling "fire."

"I heard the noise, saw a flash of light, and it was all smoky up front," the guilty radio operator said. "But it was you guys in the cockpit that declared the emergency."

"Well actually," the navigator said, "it was the copilot."

The next week someone changed the label on my squadron mailbox to "1LT Tutti Frutti."

The other pilots in the squadron were not as amused and our new squadron commander convened an emergency pilot's meeting. Lieutenant Colonel Swede had already earned a reputation for listening before talking, and started the meeting with a simple directive. "What should we be doing about this?"

"If that had been a real fire," Captain Kekumano said, "everyone on board would have been killed. Thirty minutes is enough time for a fire to eat through flight control cables or get to a fuel line."

"Doesn't even have to do that," Lieutenant Colonel Swede said, "the smoke and fumes will probably kill you first. We need to come up with an ASAP approach. Kind of like a rushed block time but damn all the speed restrictions. What do you think, Eddie?"

"I can do that, sir."

After the meeting Major Greco pulled me into his office. "Don't worry about the Tutti Frutti crap," he said. "Eddie, this is important stuff. You come up with the best way to get the airplane on the ground as soon as possible and you will be saving lives. This is the perfect job for a pilot-engineer."

I started to draw triangles in my notebook, thinking about how best to get the airplane on the ground as quickly as possible. The first step was obvious, fly V_{MO}. The "V" was for velocity and the "MO" meant "maximum operating." But at what point do you decelerate to get the landing gear down and flaps out? Start too early and you delay landing by a lot. Start too late and you can't land and are even later. But the ASAP approach was going to have to wait; we had a non-routine trip to Alaska in a few days. I picked up

Major Vandunk's navigation log, added my fuel computations, sped through the rest of the paperwork, and rushed home to get dressed for our monthly dinner with the parents. The *Lovely Mrs. Haskel* and I joined my parents and brother once a month and tonight was Mister Haskel's turn to buy. I wasn't going to be late when my dad was picking up the tab.

The morning of the trip I got to the ready room in time to see *The Nick* on the phone with his worried look, something he rarely wore. "Yeah," he said, "I know this is late notice but we need another 20,000 pounds or we aren't going anywhere. Yeah, tell them Captain Davenport screwed up but says thanks for any help." With that, he cradled the phone.

"Problem?" I asked.

He handed me Vandunk's navigation log. "Believe it or not, Lee did the entire log in statute miles. Everything is off by fifteen percent."

"Including my fuel computations."

"Yeah."

Air navigation is computed in nautical miles, not statute. A nautical mile is equal to 6,076 feet, fifteen percent more than the 5,280 feet in a statute mile. "So we didn't order enough gas then," I said. "I should have caught this."

"It was the nav's screw up," *The Nick* said.

"You took the blame just now."

"I'm the crew commander," *The Nick* said. "I own this."

It was another lesson for the notebook, but *The Nick* and I both knew who could have prevented this screw up. Me. We both knew Vandunk had to be watched and I should have realized my fuel numbers were coming up light. The pilot with the engineering degree; the guy everyone thought had a photographic memory for numbers; that guy. That was the guy who screwed up.

We flew the trip, albeit a few hours later on the first departure. If *The Nick* had any words with Vandunk, it wasn't in front of the crew. Vandunk seemed his normal, cheerful self. That night at dinner I asked if I should include a fifteen percent tip or not. "Well actually," Vandunk said, "that is what you give for exceptional service. Ten percent should be fine."

We had four days off to explore the area by day and the bars at night. I took whatever time was left over to work on the ASAP approach math. I needed a few numbers from a manual I didn't have and called back to the squadron. I was happy to hear Kevin's voice on the other end.

"Did you hear the news?" he asked.

"I guess not."

"Major Greco was fired, nobody knows why," he said. "*The Nick* is taking his place."

"But *The Nick* is just a captain," I said.

"He's the only instructor pilot in the squadron without a bust on his record," Kevin said. "Oh yeah, one more thing. You just got promoted." The promotion rate to captain for pilots is nearly 95 percent, but still it was good to have that milestone behind me. Major Greco's fall from grace was a shock.

"Yeah," *The Nick* said. "I heard that. Dan's a good guy and between you, David White, and me, he's only got three supporters in the whole squadron. You can't be mean to an entire squadron and not expect some sort of payback."

"He was fired for being mean?" I asked.

"No, he was fired for letting David do a touch and go."

"Putting a navigator in a pilot's seat is against every reg in the book," I said. "I'm surprised he would do that."

"Well we all got our weaknesses," he said. "Dan's weakness was being too good to his crew."

The Nick knew about his elevation to Crew One but was unfazed by the promotion. The next day we were pointed south, heading home.

As *The Nick* engaged the autopilot at 36,000 feet and I was preparing for the crossword puzzle marathon, I became faintly aware of a disturbance from aft of the cockpit. Just aft would be the galley, but the next compartment was where three radio operators and three teletype operators sat. They were just forward of the passenger compartment so they stayed pretty quiet, but not today.

"You smell something?" *The Nick* asked.

"Yeah," I said. "Mandy is burning dinner."

"Fire!" I turned in my seat and saw a cloud of smoke pouring from an overhead duct. *The Nick* gave me a look that telegraphed everything I needed to do.

"Mango 51," I said on the radio, "turning one-eighty, declaring an emergency, request a vector back to Elmendorf, now!"

Center accommodated us and *The Nick* pushed the nose down and the throttles forward. "Fly V$_{MO}$," I said, "and get us to 4,000 feet and 15 miles out on final. Then go idle and get dirty."

"You sure?" he asked.

"No," I said, "but I think it's going to work. I'll get the crew chiefs on the fire." I unstrapped and headed aft, but I didn't need to. Our crew chiefs were already tearing apart the overhead duct.

"It's the air conditioning, lieutenant!" The lead crew chief lifted his smoke goggle to speak. "But no flames."

"Okay," I said, "get everyone on oxygen." I returned to the cockpit and saw *The Nick* had us down below 15,000 feet. "I'm turning off the air conditioning pack."

"Do what you have to," *The Nick* said. The smoke eased up and by the time we were on final the cockpit was clear. *The Nick* asked for the landing gear at 15 miles and every notch of flaps as we hit the correct speed. We ended up ready to land two miles early.

"Not bad," *The Nick* said.

We were on the ground 15 minutes after the "Fire!" was announced. Two crewmembers and one passenger went to the hospital for smoke inhalation but were released a day later. The mechanics at Elmendorf Air Force Base tore the overhead ducts apart and found a charred rag inside the duct just aft of the galley. "If you guys had spent any more time up there it would have ignited," the maintenance officer said. "It's a good thing you got it on the ground."

The passengers returned via the airlines and the crew got another five days off in Alaska. When we got back my captain's bars were waiting in my squadron mailbox. And the "1LT TUTTI FRUTTI" label was gone.

Cabin Fires

Subtle Causes of In-Flight Fires [AC 120-80A, ¶8.]

Wiring Failures. A majority of hidden in-flight fires are the result of electrical arcs along wire bundles. In most cases, the electrical arc acts as the initiating event, igniting other surrounding materials.

Electrical Component Failures. Electrical motors can overheat, bind, fail, and possibly ignite surrounding materials. An accumulation of contaminants in the immediate area exacerbates the spread of fire in these instances.

Lightning Strikes. Although infrequent, lightning strikes have initiated fires.

Bleed Air Leaks. Aircraft with systems that use engine bleed air depend on pneumatic lines to deliver the air supply. A failure of any of these supply lines, if left unchecked, can cause high temperatures in the surrounding area.

Faulty Circuit Protection. A malfunctioning circuit breaker that does not open (trip) when it detects an abnormally high current draw may cause the affected unit or associated wiring to overheat and ignite.

Lithium Ion Batteries. Rechargeable lithium ion batteries are capable of overheating, leading to thermal runaway, which can cause the sudden release of the contents of the battery as a flaming jet, heavy smoke, unburned hydrocarbons, or in some cases the battery can explode or rocket. The resulting fire can flare repeatedly as each cell ruptures and releases its contents.

Indications of Hidden Fires [AC 120-80A, ¶9.]

Abnormal Operation or Disassociated Component Failures. Failure or uncommanded operation of an aircraft component may indicate a developing fire.

Circuit Breakers. Circuit breaker(s) tripping, especially multiple breakers such as entertainment systems or coffee makers may be an indication of damage occurring in a hidden area common to the affected components.

Hot Spots. Hot spots on the floor, sidewall, ceiling, or other panels should be immediately investigated.

Fumes. This may be one of your first indications of an impending fire. Never ignore a strange odor; you need to identify its source as soon as possible.

Visual Sighting of Smoke. Smoke coming from vents or seams between interior panels, especially from the ceiling area, is a sure sign of a problem, and you should take immediate action to determine the source.

Priority One: Get the Airplane on the Ground

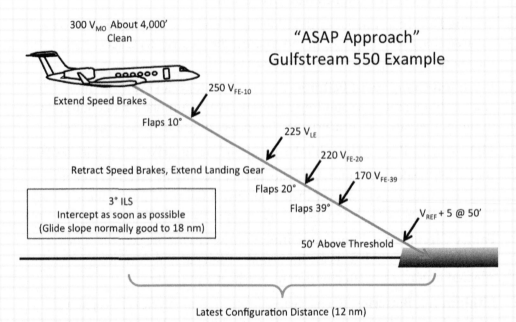

300 V_{MO} About 4,000'
Clean

Extend Speed Brakes

Flaps 10°

250 V_{FE-10}

225 V_{LE}

220 V_{FE-20}

Retract Speed Brakes, Extend Landing Gear

170 V_{FE-39}

Flaps 20°

"ASAP Approach"
Gulfstream 550 Example

3° ILS
Intercept as soon as possible
(Glide slope normally good to 18 nm)

Flaps 39°

V_{REF} + 5 @ 50'

50' Above Threshold

Latest Configuration Distance (12 nm)

[AC 120-80A, ¶13.A.] Studies have shown that a flight crew may have as few as 15-20 minutes to get an aircraft on the ground if the crew allows a hidden fire to progress without any intervention.

- Point the airplane toward the nearest runway that is long enough to get you stopped. Given a choice between more than one, an airport with an ILS would be ideal and one with fire coverage would be a good choice.

- Fly V_{MO}. If you don't put the fire out in four minutes or less, chances are you won't be able to. So you want the airplane on the ground. Don't worry about speed limitations that won't keep you from flying the airplane, i.e., 250 knots below 10,000'. Don't worry about being too heavy.

- Declare an emergency and let ATC know what you are doing, let them adjust to your needs. Ask for a vector to the nearest runway, about the weather, and approach availability. Ask for a single frequency, preferably the tower's frequency, because there may be a time when changing frequencies will be impossible. If your aircraft has a radio that is available down to the last bit of electrons on the aircraft, use it.

Flight Lessons 2: Advanced Flight

- Get the ILS tuned and the autopilot in control as soon as possible. (An LPV would be a good second choice.) Even with EVAS there can be a point where programming the FMS and tuning the radios will become difficult if you can't see them. Once the autopilot has the runway in its electronic grasp, you can have it land the airplane even if you don't have an auto land system. If you lose sight of the instruments, let the autopilot do its thing and once you feel runway below you, apply the brakes.

- Get to know how late you need to configure to get the gear down and enough flaps to get the airplane stopped. In the G450, for example, you can fly V_{MO} to about 17 miles, dial in VREF so the throttles come to idle, pull the speed brakes, select 10° flaps at 250 KCAS, select 20° flaps at 220 KCAS, retract the speed brakes, extend the landing gear, and select 39° flaps at 180 KCAS.

- Get to know where your critical controls and switches are by feel. You should know how to extend the landing gear by touch only. The same, obviously, is true with the flaps. Not all critical systems are so obvious. In many Gulfstreams, for example, the switch used to arm the ground spoilers are in different places. In the G450 the answer is to put your hand on MCDU #3, feel aft for the six switches, and feel for the guarded switch furthest aft and right.

- If you have a chance, discuss post landing duties with the other pilot and other available crewmembers. Decide which exit is best, where to funnel passengers — upwind on the grass is best — and who will secure the aircraft. Let tower know where you plan on sending passengers so fire rescue doesn't run anyone over.

- Put the airplane on the ground. Most aircraft can survive a no flare landing and that may be best for energy dissipation. Practice all of this in the simulator.

Priority Two: Fight the Fire (if you can)

[AC 120-80A, ¶14.]

Flight crewmembers must don smoke goggles and oxygen masks at the first indication of smoke or fumes and before accomplishing any abnormal or emergency procedures associated with smoke or fume elimination in accordance with your company's approved procedures and/or the manufacturer's recommendations. Any delay might result in a crewmembers' inability to breathe and/or see.

The flight crew's best defense against smoke and fumes is the quick donning of oxygen masks and associated smoke goggles. If you are required to leave the flight deck to assist in fighting a cabin fire, the FAA recommends that you don a PBE before leaving the flight deck. If you are to assist in an evacuation, you should don a PBE if you suspect that there is smoke or fumes in the cabin.

Recommended Procedures.

Immediately don protective equipment

Plan for an immediate descent and landing at the nearest suitable airport

Do not use smoke/fume elimination procedures to treat a fire

[AC 120-80A, ¶15.]

Be aggressive; if flames are visible, fight the fire immediately

If flames are not visible, find the base or source of the fire

Do not reset CBs, unless required for safe flight

Relocate passengers as necessary

Locate hot spots using the back of your hand

Don PBE

When searching for the source of a fire, open storage compartments or doors very carefully

5: Lefty

Haskel by his trusty EC-135J in Brunei (Eddie's collection)

We stood awkwardly in front of the commander's office, all thinking the same thing. "Who screwed up?"

It was the obvious question. Lieutenant Colonel Swede called the four of us to his office. Walt Kekumano was the only missing copilot; he was in Okinawa on the weekly rotation. It was left unsaid that Kevin Davies would do the talking if we were in as a collective. He had the most time in the squadron and then came me. But in terms of rank, Captains Bernie Palmer and Dan Martin had us both beat.

"Awfully quiet in there." Bernie whispered. "I heard he keeps the stool in there for Chinese water torture. Somebody is going to talk."

Just down the hall, the front door to the building opened and in walked the squadron commander. The four of us exchanged embarrassed glances.

"Sorry to keep you guys waiting," Colonel Swede said as he fumbled with his office keys, "Come on in. Take any seat you can find." We shuffled in. The other three found regular chairs; I was left with the wooden stool.

"I've already had a talk with Walt on the phone and I wanted to see you four before I told the rest of the squadron," he said while leaning against his desk. He looked at our faces and rethought his stance, taking the chair from behind his desk to the front. "We are about to lose three aircraft commanders and I think the other two will be leaving within a year. Walt is just about done with the upgrade program but I am still short four. That means I need all four of you copilots to upgrade as soon as possible." The four of us let out a collective sigh of relief. Bernie and Dan had the look of paroled death row inmates, but Kevin looked more worried than before. I diverted my eyes to avoid drawing attention to my pilot training classmate.

"It takes about two months to upgrade," Colonel Swede continued. "Kevin you have the necessary hours and you are senior in EC-135 experience. So you go first." He paused for a reaction but got none. "Eddie, I'm sorry but you just don't have the hours yet so you go last. That's just the price for being the youngster in the group."

"I understand, sir." I'd have to wait eight months to upgrade, but that was still a full year ahead of schedule. "I hope I have the hours by then."

"We'll make sure you do," Swede said. "So that's it then: Kevin, Bernie, Dan, and then Eddie. Thanks guys." He got up and shook our hands and we filed out. I fell into line according to the new pecking order and was last to the door. "Eddie," Colonel Swede said, "can we talk a little longer?" I nodded and took a regular seat, leaving the stool behind.

"Do you think Kevin's going to punch?" he asked.

"I don't know, sir. Kevin plays his cards close to his chest."

"Yeah," he said. "He's a good safety officer but it's curious that he timed his safety school to run out on exactly the same day his four-year pilot training commitment ends. He already has his two years on station so I'm taking a bit of a risk upgrading him."

"Yes sir," I said, "it would be a loss for the squadron." I left it unsaid that Kevin and I graduated on the same day. My two years on station would be in March, just a year away.

"You are the one I'm worried about," he said, as if reading my mind.

"Sir?"

"Your engineering degree is making you raw meat for the assignment process," he said. "I got a call from the Air Force test pilot school last week and from the Pentagon a week before that. They're all waiting for your two-year point."

"I guess it's good to have options," I said, "but I was hoping to have more time here."

"I can make that happen," Colonel Swede said, "but you have to trust me. I have a plan for you Eddie, and it means another three years on the island of your birth." Oahu wasn't the island of my birth; it was the island of my youth. But close enough. "Do we have an understanding, Eddie?"

"Yes, sir."

The squadron geared up to churn out aircraft commanders, which meant those of us not in the business of instructing or being instructed had nothing to do. Walt took over Crew Five, which was great news, but since he wasn't an instructor we never flew. I became a frequent visitor to the base library where I found a particularly interesting British science magazine ad that said they would send me all the parts and some instructions to build my very own computer, all for 79 pounds and 50 p.

The kit arrived a month later and I got to work with my trusty soldering iron. The computer hooked up to a television and was programmed with eight switches, hardly user friendly but it worked and was my very first real computer. Later issues of the British magazine helped me to construct a keyboard and a visit to our local electronics store solved the issue of program storage. My set up was complete, a portable television set, my computer on a printed circuit board, my keyboard made from an old typewriter and paperclips, and a portable cassette tape recorder.

The ensemble was too large to take on trips, so it was with mixed feelings I found our crew finally scheduled to fly. "Vandunk's mind is not in the game," Walt said as I made my way to the flight plan vault, "check everything twice." When was his mind ever in the game?

While Vandunk managed to keep the log in nautical miles this time, he got the magnetic variation backwards from start to finish. That changed all the courses and after throwing in the wind it changed most of the air nautical distances. It took me most of the night to fix and all of my self-restraint to not say anything to the major.

We flew the trip and Vandunk either didn't notice or didn't care that his log was filled with erasures and someone else's handwriting. The trip was routine except for the return leg from Japan. "The admiral is complaining about his ears," the flight attendant reported. "He says you guys are being too rough with the power or something like that."

Walt and I stared at the four throttles, which had pretty much been set for the last hour. "I've never used the manual pressurization system," I said, "you?"

"It's an emergency procedure," Walt said. "Is this an emergency?"

"No," I said.

"Well I guess we leave it alone then." Walt returned to the newspaper he was reading and I returned to my fuel logs. When we got home we added "erratic automatic pressurization system" to our maintenance log. The next week we heard the fix was, "could not duplicate, aircraft returned to service."

At our next squadron meeting Kevin was congratulated for completing the upgrade to aircraft commander and it was announced that Captain Bernie Palmer was next to move to the left seat. The applause was subdued and I sensed many of the enlisted crewmembers looking my way. Bernie had only been in the squadron about six months whereas I had easily a year more time on station. Of course Bernie had two more years as a pilot and had 1,500 hours needed to upgrade. I was nearing 1,200.

With another month with nothing to do, I soon discovered my homemade computer could do subroutines, making it much more useful. A subroutine is a small packet of computer code that can be reused over and over again. I wrote a subroutine that turned a starting and ending latitude and longitude into a course line and distance; and then another to turn all that into time and fuel. Before long I had the ability to check Vandunk's flight plan in less time than it took him to write it. I was on to something.

The squadron bought its first computer and parked it in the mission ready room, an object of curiosity until the radio operators discovered the fun of solitaire. I competed for time, trying to load my takeoff data, fuel log, and navigation programs. Once the navigators got wind of what I was doing, they ran full time interference, threatening violence to anyone who would detract me from my goal of replacing Vandunk with a computer program. In another two months, I was done.

"Time to upgrade, Eddie."

Walt was picked to upgrade to instructor pilot, which meant a return to the right seat. I moved to the left seat, he instructed, and another instructor sat in the jump seat to instruct us both. Since Walt had only made the jump from right to left earlier that year, all of his lessons were perfect. Even with the nose wheel.

Most guys really struggled with the nose wheel tiller. The Boeing 707 doesn't have a tiller on the right side of the cockpit and a new aircraft commander will never experience it until moving to the left seat. The tiller is mounted vertically and the nose wheel pivots horizontally; so the tiller's movement doesn't translate in one's mind. I turned the tiller and the entire airplane jerked to one side, shuddering in complaint.

"Don't move the tiller with an eye to making the nose wheel move," he said. "Apply pressure and see what happens, then adjust."

That was just what I needed to hear. Every step of the way Walt recalled his own struggles with the switch from the right to the left seat and that made my own transformation that much easier. For every hurdle, there was a story. "I imagine my right foot on the taxi line and that seems to keep the nose wheel where it needs to be." That worked.

And so it went with each lesson until the day I upgraded. "Grasshopper no more," *The Nick* said as he signed my upgrade orders. "I need to get serious with you for just a minute, Eddie."

"This will be a first," I said.

"Yeah," he said, laughing. "Everything you've learned in the last two months was just the mechanical side of flying the airplane from another seat and the extra stuff we expect from aircraft commanders. The most important part of the left seat is what you already knew and you'll get a chance to further develop. That's how you treat the crew. You are going to make mistakes, don't let that bother you. You need to learn from those mistakes."

"I've learned from the worst," I said. "And the best," I added.

The Nick got up and patted me on the back, signaling the evaluation was complete. "Young Eddie-san is now samurai."

The Left Seat (For the first time)

Proper Seat Position

Find a way to ensure your eyes are in the same place everytime you sit in the seat. This will be critical when it comes to taxi, takeoff, and landing. Generally speaking, further forward increases your perceived visibility over the nose. Your manufacturer may have specific recommendations.

Wheel Brake Technique

Larger aircraft have more inertia and brakes can seem "grabby" to pilots not used to so much mass. Remember to gently apply pressure (as opposed to pedal deflection) and wait for a response. Keeping your heels on the floor for landing will avoid an inadvertent brake application on touchdown, which can slam the nose down hard enough to break something.

Tiller Technique

Aircraft with nose wheel tillers require finesse to avoid jerkiness. Remember to apply gentle pressure (as opposed to tiller deflection) left and right and wait for a response.

Nose Wheel Placement

Find a long, straight taxiway line to line up on and have an outside observer confirm you are on centerline. Look for a reference point on your glareshield or the nose of the aircraft that lines up with your eyes. Remember there will be paralax from your seated position to the left of the aircraft's center. (There could also be paralax created by the windshield's thickness.) Alternatively, some pilots line up their knees or feet with where they perceive the centerline to be.

Main Gear Placement

You can get a pretty good idea of where your main gear are from the cockpit by learning their relationship to the limit of your vision from the seated position:

1. Align your eyes to your normal sitting position.

2. Have another pilot stand outside, abeam your eyes, with a cell phone.

3. Have the pilot inch to and from the aircraft until you can just barely see his or her feet on the ground.

4. Ask the pilot to remain in that position.

5. Leave the cockpit and compare the location of the pilot's feet to the track of the main gear. That is how much space you have between the limits of your vision from the seated position to the main gear wheels.

Taxi the Entire Airplane

Study your aircraft's top view diagrams to determine where aircraft extremities will be during a minimum radius turn. In many aircraft the wing tips or tail describe an arc greater than the nose of the airplane and tight turns must consider these radii. When in doubt, stop the airplane, set the parking brake, and get wing walkers. Taxi lines are often painted for smaller aircraft and some

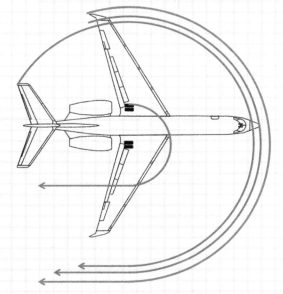

aircraft can confuse marshallers. A GV's wings, for example, describe an arc wider than the tail, unlike the GIV.

Landing on Runway Centerline

Pilots used to landing from the right seat tend to land on the left side of the runway when landing from the left seat. The easy fix is to be aware of the tendency and to remind yourself "centerline!" on every landing until the tendency disappears.

Judging Braking Effort

There is only one thing worse than braking too hard and then having to add power to make the next exit and that is not braking hard enough and running out of runway. But if you are landing on a shorter than usual runway, how do you judge distance remaining versus your normal deceleration? Try looking for the next runway distance remaining marker and multiply that by 20 to come up with a speed that gives you a gentle deceleration, by 30 for one that means you need to get serious about stopping, and by 40 for a wakeup call that means you have to start worrying about the anti-skid.

Let's say, for example, you look up and see the "3" which means you have 3,000 feet remaining.

- If you are now doing 3 x 20 = 60 knots, you are in great shape and will probably be able to coast to the end.

- If you are doing 3 x 30 = 90 knots, you need to get more aggressive with the brakes.

- If you are doing 3 x 40 = 120 knots, you really need to get on the brakes or you will have a CDM (Career Defining Moment).

Getting Over the New Captain Syndrome

Nobody is more aware of your status as a new captain than you. That is to say, most everyone else is not aware at all unless you do something or say something that lets them know that. A few pointers:

- Crewmembers and passengers need to know somebody is in charge and that somebody knows what is going on. That person is you. Sometimes the "cool and calm" demeanor is an act, but it is a necessary act.

- The goofy "one of the guys" persona favored by some copilots doesn't work for a captain. Passengers don't want to think their captain is mortal and they can be unnerved to find just how young you really are.

- Younger crewmembers are like passengers in some ways, they don't want to think of you as incredibly young and inexperienced. You need to act the part for them too.

- Your fellow captains have been through this transition before and will be a great source of advice.

- A good captain takes crew resource management seriously. Retake your initial CRM courses again, armed with your new perspective. Remember a good captain sets the right tone from the very first crew briefing, listens to the opinions of the crew, delegates tasks fairly, and makes decisions that are easy to understand and implement.

- A good captain is human and makes mistakes. That is why self critique and crew critiques are so important.

- A good captain ends every briefing with questions that encourage crew participation and stimulate alternative views. "Do you have any questions or comments?" "Am I forgetting anything?"

6: Fly Safe

Air Force Mishap Investigation Course (USAF Photo)

As the squadron's newest aircraft commander, things had hardly changed for me. I was leading a crew of one, still without a copilot or a navigator. The other crews were fully manned until Kevin put his papers in to separate on November 29th, 1983, four years to the day after we both got our wings.

"You couldn't be any more obvious," I said the next time I saw him.

"The Air Force isn't for me," he said, "you know that."

"Yeah," I said. "You were destined for the airlines on day one."

"I'm sorry, Eddie."

"Why?" I asked.

"Guess who has orders to safety school?"

"That's not so bad," I said.

"You get a two year commitment," he said, "by that time you will be too old for the airlines."

That was true. The entire system was designed around Air Force or Navy pilots getting their wings at 22 or 23 years of age, paying the military back with four years of service, and going civilian no older than 27. I had just turned 26. In two years I would be too old.

I thought I would have to break the news gently to the *Lovely Mrs. Haskel.* I was wrong.

"You don't want to be an airline pilot Eddie," she said.

"I don't?"

"You would be bored senseless," she said. "Besides, think of all the time in front of an audience you get. All those briefings."

"Kind of weird," I said. "For an introvert like me."

"You aren't an introvert," she said. I left her point undisputed.

The next day Lieutenant Colonel Swede tried to sell me on the school, not knowing I had already decided it was a good thing. "Eddie," he said, "this puts you a cut above everyone else, this school is a big deal."

"I know, sir."

"As an engineer you will ace it. This also means you get another year in Hawaii," he added.

"That's great, sir."

"Now most safety officers don't get to fly much," he said, "but that won't be the case with you. You're going to fly more now than ever. We have a big turnover coming."

I left his office and heard my name from down the hall, from the scheduling office. "Westpac with Crew One," the scheduler said. "You leave tomorrow."

Looking at the carnage on the scheduling board, Colonel Swede's words were validated. *The Nick* was leaving in a month, off to Northwest Airlines. Walt Kekumano was already gone, working for the Pacific Air Forces Headquarters staff on base. All told we had four pilots leaving and three coming in.

"Five pilots leaving," the scheduler said. "Look at the top line."

I elevated my gaze upward. Lieutenant Colonel Swede would be gone in a month. "The Pentagon," the scheduler said. "What the five-sided puzzle palace wants, the five-sided puzzle palace gets."

The next day I sat in the left seat, reviewing paperwork as the rest of the crew got the bird ready to fly. Captain Carl Gifford's navigation log was flawless as was Lieutenant Jon Patrick's fuel log. "Here are the aircraft forms, sir."

"Jon," I said, "I've been a captain barely a year. You don't need to call me sir."

Flying with Crew One was always a treat; everyone knew what they were doing and things got done with less drama. Our aircraft was 62-3584, our oldest but usually most reliable. We were climbing through eight or nine thousand feet when that notion came to an abrupt end. "Fire light, number three," Jon said. I scanned the row of engine gauges and didn't see any other problems, just the fire light.

"Engine fire during flight checklist," I said, keeping the aircraft climbing. "Nav, where is the tanker?"

"He's just hitting the orbit right now," Carl said, "you want me to call him?"

"Yeah," I said, "tell him we won't be needing him today." I pulled the number three lever to idle and started the stopwatch on my panel. "Checklist, please."

"Throttle cut-off, unless needed."

"Jon," I said, "I've pulled the number three throttle to idle thirty seconds ago, the fire light remains on. Please confirm I have my hand on the correct throttle."

"You really going to shut it down?" he asked.

"Yes," I said, "confirm it please."

"That's the one," he said. I pulled the throttle up and over the cut-off detent and we watched the engine indications wind to zero.

"Fire switch," he said, "pull if required."

"The light remains on," I said, "confirm I have my hand on the correct switch." He did and I pulled the fire switch. We declared an emergency, turned around and landed where we started. The trip was delayed a day and we were assigned another aircraft.

When we got back from the Westpac the news around the squadron was that 62-3584 was fine; maintenance could not find anything wrong. "I flew 584 on a training flight yesterday," Bernie said, "no sign of engine fires."

"The book says shut it down," I said.

"I know," he said, "I'm just saying."

"Saying what?" I thought, but did not say. Bernie was an excellent pilot but not the most articulate.

Two weeks later Bernie was given command of Crew One, the top spot in the squadron. He took the next week off to visit family in Virginia and I was again with Crew One going Westpac on aircraft 62-3584.

"Not again," I heard from the right seat. I looked down to see our now familiar fire light.

"Engine fire during flight checklist," I said.

"Really?"

We shut the engine down and I spent the next few minutes explaining the Pratt and Whitney TF33-P-9 fire detection system to Jon and Carl. The fire detection system was nothing more than 10 temperature sensors in each engine and pylon with no fault detection. If a light came on, one of those sensors was either detecting a fire or was broken. But we had no way of knowing if the light was reporting fact or fiction so the flight manual said the engine must be shut down.

"But the EGT was okay," Jon said.

"The exhaust gas temperature is only a measure of what is seen in the tail pipe," I said, "it measures what some people call the hot section. It is designed to be on fire, after all. We have to worry about the cold section. That's where the raw fuel and hydraulic fluid is. If that stuff catches on fire, we lose the engine and if it goes catastrophically, there is a chance we can lose the wing." As I articulated the systems my faith in my decision solidified.

We put the airplane down, waited a day, and flew the trip on another bird. Maintenance once again stamped the records with the infamous, "CND" or could not duplicate, and returned the airplane to service. The day after that, 62-3584 flew a training mission with no problems.

When we got back from our week in west Asia the squadron had a new commander and a new second in command. The new boss was Lieutenant Colonel Jerry Spindler, an RC-135 pilot turned staff officer from Air Force headquarters in Korea. His second, the director of operations, was Major William Condit, a pilot from our sister squadron in North Dakota. William came with a good reputation; Colonel Spindler was an unknown quantity. The RC-135 is a similar airplane but with a completely different mission. We flew people from Point A to Point B. The RC-135 is a spy plane that flew along the border of the Soviet Union to eavesdrop with sophisticated electronic equipment. The "R" in RC-135 stood for reconnaissance. The "E" in EC-135 stood for electronic but was a slight of hand used to disguise the real mission. We filed into the squadron briefing room for our first glimpse of the man.

The 9th ACCS could never muster more than four-fifths of its total number, given that one crew was always on the road. But we managed to assemble about a hundred crewmembers that day into our briefing room. At the front stood the new boss. He was a balding and overweight officer with gray, wire brush eyebrows that singled him out as the oldest person in the room. We may have had a radio operator or two with larger guts, but certainly no officer.

"It is an honor to be your commander," he started. "I think you will find I am a typical crew dog. I get along with everyone and the thing I care about most is the skill and professionalism we each show flying the airplane. Now you are probably wondering about my leadership style. So I copied this out of my favorite text book and you can read it better than I can say it."

He placed an acetate slide over a projector positioned in the middle of the room and flipped a switch. It was a page of text from an officership manual I remembered from my days as an Air Force Reserve Officer Training Corps cadet. We sat quietly and read as he read with equal silence. I was seated in the front row and could barely make out the text.

"So let's get on with the business of flying," he said at last. "I came from RC-135s, planes with real missions. We were on the pointy edge of the gun." I stifled a laugh at his botched metaphor. "I plan to show each of you how it's done, the right way. We'll have no more novice pilots aborting missions flying perfectly good airplanes. You got that Captain Haskel?"

"I'm not so sure, sir." I said.

"In my office," he said, "now. Squadron dismissed."

When you are getting yelled at as an airman or young sergeant, the person doing the yelling is given free reign of the airspace and the person being yelled at is in what some call "the brace." You are to stand at attention, your eyes caged forward, motionless. It was deemed unseemly for an officer, but that's how I spent the next ten minutes.

"Don't you have anything to say?" he asked.

"I will follow the rule of law in the flight manual," I said, "unless presented with compelling evidence that it is unsafe to do so, sir."

"I think you don't have the common sense to fly one of my airplanes," he said. "I'm taking you off your crew. Oh, you think you're going to safety school? You aren't. Dismissed."

Strangely, the only emotion I felt was embarrassment. Having to explain you've been fired to everyone you know has to be shaming, even if unjustly. Fired is fired.

I saluted, did an about face, and opened the door to an empty hallway with a solitary figure poking his head out of the next office. "Eddie," he said, "come in here." I followed Major Condit into his office and he closed the door behind us.

"You lay low for a few days," he said, "I'll calm the boss down. You kind of shot him in the face in front of the entire squadron on his first day. You can't blame him for being upset."

"I see your point, sir," I said. I had to wonder why I was blind to that very fact with an audience looking on; my intuition had failed me.

I left his office and found the squadron devoid of all other pilots. The only clue was a note in my mailbox. "Come to the golf course bar, we need to talk." I showed up and found a few of the squadron pilots had organized a training session and I was the guest speaker.

"We need to know what you know," Dan Martin said as the others eyed me intently. "What happens if we don't shut the engine down with a fire light?" The table was covered with a disposable paper with just the words "Derek!" written upside-down in double ink by our waiter. I pulled out a pen and started to draw. As I covered each facet of the engine fire detection system the concepts solidified and my confidence grew. Each pilot agreed there was no choice in the matter: a fire light equals engine shut down.

The next week my orders to safety school showed up with instructions to visit the colonel in charge of the Pacific Air Forces Headquarters safety office. The colonel said he just wanted to instill in me the importance of what I was doing. It wasn't an excuse to party for three months, I had to take it seriously.

"I will," I said.

"And don't wash out," he said. "No pilot likes math, but you are just going to have to study hard."

"I like math," I said.

"Sure you do," he said. I left his office and tried to navigate myself to the front of the building, where I entered, but somehow ended up in the back where I ran into newly promoted Major K. Walter Kekumano.

"Eddie," he said, "your name was in lights up here last week."

"Me?"

"Yeah." Walter's goofy grin forecast more to come. "Your new squadron commander had your safety school orders canceled but didn't give a reason. The safety office demanded he replace you with another pilot with an engineering degree and he gave them Bernie."

"Bernie's a history major," I said.

"Yeah," Walt said. "The staff cut Bernie's orders but somebody finally figured that out. Now they think Spindler is either an idiot or a liar."

"I wouldn't rule out both," I said.

"Well you be careful, Eddie." He lowered his voice. "You made him look pretty stupid and he's going to get even."

I thought about that for a day or two, thinking of a dozen answers better than "I'm not so sure, sir." Years ago, in prisoner of war training, I came away from a beating after saying something I thought was funny to a guard who didn't agree. Some thoughts are best unspoken.

I had three months in San Bernardino, California to consider my sins while learning everything there was to know about being an aircraft mishap investigator. Most of my classmates were from the bomb-dropping, missile-launching part of the Air Force and many of them struggled with the math. Me? I struggled with every course dealing with pilot psychology.

We began the course with a self assessment and ended it with another by a board-certified psychiatrist. The shrink pronounced my self assessment to be rubbish. "You are the classic ESTP," he said. The tests showed me to be an extraverted, sensing, thinking, and perceiving human being.

The good news was that I fit the Air Force model for future command precisely. The bad news was that, apparently, I didn't know who I was.

James Albright

Pilot Psychology

[From various sources, including myersbriggs.org, adapted for pilots.]

Personality types can be broken down into four personality preferences. For the purposes of pilot psychology, the profiles can be used to teach individual pilots about their own strengths and weaknesses as well as hints on how to improve crew resource management techniques.

The first step is to determine your personality profile with one of each of the four preferences. You end up with a letter for each preference that can describe you in four letters, such as "ESTP" or "INFJ" for two examples.

Personality Preferences ("Favorite World")

Extraversion -- You are talkative, outgoing, like to work out ideas with others and think aloud, and like to be the center of attention.

Introversion -- You are reserved, quiet, like to contemplate and think things through, and you prefer to observe rather than occupy the attention center.

Personality Preferences (Information)

Sensing -- You focus on the reality of how things are, pay attention to facts, prefer practical ideas, and describe things in a literal way.

i**N**tuition -- You like to imagine how things can be, you enjoy ideas as concepts, and you describe things figuratively.

Personality Preferences (Decisions)

Thinking -- You make decisions dispassionately, using logic, you value fairness and enjoy finding flaws in arguments.

Feeling -- You make decisions based on your feelings, you value harmony and forgiveness, you are empathetic.

Personality Preferences (Structure)

Judging -- You like having things settled, you think rules should be followed and deadlines met, you make and follow plans.

Perceiving -- You like keeping your options open, you think rules and deadlines are flexible, you like to improvise.

Personality Preference Strengths and Weaknesses

Each personality preference has its strengths and weakness, In terms of pilots, some of these may be as follows:

Extraversion. Pilot strengths: stimulates communications on the flight deck, brings out ideas and solutions from the team. Pilot weaknesses: may overwhelm other crewmembers with personality, can cause others to withdraw.

Introversion. Pilot strengths: can come up with solutions to complex problems and avoid pitfalls from tricky situations. Pilot weaknesses: may intimidate junior crewmembers or "underwhelm" those senior.

Sensing. Pilot strengths: can take in lots of information and apply technical solutions. Pilot weaknesses: can miss "outside the box" solutions that solve problems beyond what is given in the flight manual.

Intuition. Pilot strengths: can tap into a broad range of experiences to come up with ideas others would miss. Pilot weaknesses: might miss standard, workable solutions while contemplating others, can "miss the trees for the forest."

Thinking. Pilot strengths: usually gets the problem solved right, the first time. Pilot weaknesses: might alienate others while striving for technical perfection, can "win the battle but lose the war" when dealing with fellow crewmembers. The brain has many congnitive limits, some you may not be aware of. Do not discount the power of intuition to overcome many of these limits.

Feeling. Pilot strengths: brings the best out of the crew, encourages others to contribute and may produce solutions any one individual would have missed. Pilot weaknesses: can miss obvious, technical solutions, sometimes "all of us are dumber than one of us."

Judging. Pilot strengths: less prone to making mistakes, tend to get things done as they had been practiced and flight tested. Pilot weaknesses: may fail to improvise when problems are compounded or outside the known envelope of solutions.

Perceiving. Pilot strengths: able to improvise and come up with solutions to complex problems and multiple emergencies. Pilot weaknesses: prone to making mistakes when ignoring tried and true solutions.

Pilot Adaptation Strategies

Extraverted pilots should realize they could overwhelm others who are not so outgoing. If the other pilot fails to engage at the same level, be willing to "tone it down." When trying to solve problems, ask questions that require more than a yes or no. Instead of "have you ever seen this before?" try "what do you think is going on here?" Introverted pilots should realize that others with outgoing personalities may be uncomfortable with silence and may need to voice their thoughts as a part of their problem-solving method. Realize they may take your silence as hostility and you may need to set them at ease. "That's pretty interesting, give me a minute or two to think about that."

Sensing pilots should realize that problems can sometimes masquerade as problems of another kind, that some problems have never been before catalogued, or that their memories can fade. If the other pilot has an intuitive idea, you should entertain it fully before responding with cold, hard facts. If your initial ideas were wrong, you may never get a course correction if you don't allow the other pilot to speak up. Intuitive pilots should realize that sometimes a problem does come right out of the flight manual and that the obvious answer is the right one. If the other pilot is spring-loaded to the text book answer don't shut the idea down but offer suggestions in the form of a question. "I can see that, but what about this?"

Thinking pilots should realize that the "egg head" approach can force feeling pilots to withdraw, for fear of looking stupid. Spouting out the right answer immediately can shut down the other pilot's creative side and rob you of any ideas from that pilot that you might have overlooked. Feeling pilots should realize that some problems do not permit long think sessions and that the quick solution might be right. They should also realize the other pilot's book knowledge can be flawed and sometimes another view is needed.

Judging pilots must realize that the other pilot's improvisational approaches can yield fruit now and then and should be entertained as time permits. If convinced your solution is the correct one, try convincing the other pilot with a little praise for the alternative. "That would work well in some cases, but in this case the book answer might just do the trick." Perceiving pilots should realize they can be seen as sloppy or unknowing by other pilots. Sometimes it is best to start an idea with an admission it is "coloring outside the lines" or by verbalizing the book answer. "I know the book says A but maybe we should consider B."

7: Pressure

Two EC-135J's from T-33 (USAF Photo)

After three months of combing through aircraft wreckage and researching just how badly things in aviation can get, I looked forward to getting back to the business of flying airplanes. I rushed into the squadron the morning after my return from the mainland, forgetting the squadron rarely got up before 7 a.m. I waited in the squadron ready room, wanting to be the first when the scheduler showed up to unlock his office. Captain Bernie Palmer was the second pilot to enter the squadron that morning and was unhappy to see me.

"Eddie," he said, "let's get some coffee. You can't be here cold turkey."

"English," I said, "Bernie I communicate with English."

"Intel," Bernie said, "you need to catch up on the last three months if you want to survive."

I hopped into the right seat of Bernie's Datsun 240Z and we sped out of the parking lot just as Lieutenant Colonel Spindler was entering. Spindler shot me a glance. "Just made it," Bernie said, "you owe me."

"The week after you left," Bernie began, "Colonel Spindler ordered every pilot in for a meeting and he talked about how he was going to fly on every trainer until he was satisfied we all measured up to his standards. But until then we would have to fly all the trips."

"His standards?" I said. "Is he any good?"

"No," Bernie said. "But that's not the problem. Well, it is a problem but that's not your problem. See, the next week we ran out of pilots so Spindler had to fly the Westpac with my crew on 62-3584. You know that fire light?"

"Yeah."

"It turns out it was a burner can working its way loose," he said. "It only happened when the airplane was heavy and the engine was at full power for a long time."

"Like on a Westpac with a full load of people flying to meet a tanker."

"You got it," he said. "Well they got that light and Jon and Carl begged him to shut down the engine and he said no. They showed up behind the tanker when the boom operator said, 'hey you guys are trailing a lot of smoke behind your number three engine.' So he finally agreed to turn back to Honolulu but still didn't shut down the engine."

"He's lucky if that's all that happened."

"There's more," Bernie said. "Jon tells the colonel that you always declared an emergency."

"I did."

"Well that was all he needed to hear to not declare an emergency. So they ended up on final approach to runway eight left and got sent around. When Spindler pushed the throttles forward number three exploded right off the wing and ended up in Keehi Lagoon. It fell within a few feet of a luxury yacht full of people. They're lucky they didn't kill anyone. The Navy pax refuse to fly with him anymore."

I sat quietly and grinned.

"You got that German thing," he said, "don't you?"

"Shadenfreude," I said, "and yes, I got that."

"So the base goes ballistic and Spindler says the problem was you never wrote up the engine correctly and that as our safety officer you should have impounded the airplane."

"Nobody's going to buy that," I said.

"Nobody does," Bernie said, "but that's the story Spindler is telling everyone. So you be careful. Oh, one more thing." He paused, as if saving the best for last. "You got assigned the newest copilot and navigator in the squadron. The copilot is Lieutenant Jim Dellums. He seems pretty sharp. The navigator is a piece of work. They are already calling him 'wrong way.' His last name is Wong."

"I know him," I said. "The name is charitable." I had flown with Calvin Wong back in tankers where his claim to fame was confusing north with south and forgetting what a standard 12-hour clock looks like. We learned to deal with his radar formation calls by insisting he add the words "left" or "right" to all his reports. As in, "receiver is at your left 3 o'clock position."

"How did Wong ever pass the special duty screening?" I asked.

"That's another thing," Bernie said. "The squadron lost its special duty status. We are now just a run of the mill unit. Wong's dream sheet had been in the system for two years but he never made the cut. Now there is no cut and he works for you."

"Ordinarily I would have a problem with any navigator being called 'Wrong Way' and in the case of a Chinese-American doubly so," I said "But in Calvin's case, 'Wrong Way Wong' pretty much sums it up."

Bernie was satisfied that I was sufficiently informed and drove us back to the squadron. I was happy to see the scheduling board had Crew Five fully manned with its first trip on the board. We were going to San Diego, California for a few days and then to Sacramento for a few more. It would be an ideal way to get to know the new copilot and learn if Calvin had finally learned to navigate.

I tried and failed to open the navigators' office safe, but a passing navigator I didn't recognize took pity and opened it for me. She wore senior navigator wings and our squadron patch, which would make her the first female officer in the squadron's history. I introduced myself but was stopped in midsentence.

"I know who you are," she said.

"Who am I?" I asked.

"You are a navigator's best friend," she said. "And you are the squadron's worst kept secret." She handed me my trip folder, locked the safe and left. She never completed her side of the introduction ritual. Things went better with the new copilot and Calvin seemed like Calvin.

That evening the *Lovely Mrs. Haskel* was anxious to hear all about the new crew and I waxed poetic about the copilot. "Jim has the steely-eyed pilot look down cold! He is articulate, his paperwork was perfect, and it sounds like he knows his stuff. If there was an Air Force recruiting poster for copilots, he would be a fine model. I think I am going to call him Captain Steve Canyon."

"Not him," the *Lovely Mrs. Haskel* said, "I asked you about that asshole Wong."

The *Lovely Mrs. Haskel* didn't often resort to profanity, but I had long ago noticed that anyone with a track record of trying to kill me was quickly elevated to asshole status.

"Seems about the same," I said, "but he has to have learned something over the last three years. Besides next week all we have to do is find California. We just head east and turn left."

"Yes," she said, "but on the way back you have to pick out a small island in the middle of the world's largest ocean." I had to concede she had a point.

The next week we were flying from San Diego to Sacramento with an airplane full of Navy passengers. The flight to California was uneventful. Captain Wong ceded all navigation responsibility to the squadron's computer and to the airplane's three inertial navigation systems. Copilot Dellums' radio procedures were perfect and his instrument approach was right out of the

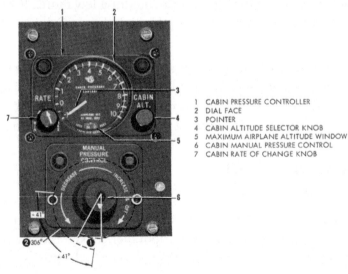

1 CABIN PRESSURE CONTROLLER
2 DIAL FACE
3 POINTER
4 CABIN ALTITUDE SELECTOR KNOB
5 MAXIMUM AIRPLANE ALTITUDE WINDOW
6 CABIN MANUAL PRESSURE CONTROL
7 CABIN RATE OF CHANGE KNOB

textbook. After spending fewer than ten hours in flight with him, I decided he might be the squadron's top copilot.

I engaged the autopilot once we had leveled off at 35,000 feet. The navigation system was locked on one set of coordinates to the next. "Navigator, copilot," Dellums said.

"Rawgh," Wong said, pronouncing "Roger" in a single syllable.

"I think you entered east instead of west on waypoint seven," Dellums said.

"Rawgh," Wong said.

"What does that mean?" Dellums asked.

I flipped to waypoint seven in time to see the longitude change from east to west. Dellums really was Steve Canyon. I sat back in my seat, happily realizing I might actually be able to relax on trips for a change. With my head tilted back I closed my eyes for a few seconds, thinking about our destination. McClellan Air Force Base was in northeast Sacramento and home to a squadron of WC-135's, a Boeing 707 designed to take air samples from nuclear airbursts. It was a good destination for us since we could always find a mechanic and it was close enough to Napa Valley to make a wine tasting trip a possibility.

I opened my eyes and turned my head to the right only to see Dellums gently rotating the manual pressurization controller over his head. It was an emergency procedure using an emergency system I had never touched. "Watcha doing?" I asked, trying to be casual about the whole thing.

"Pax are saying they are feeling pressure bumps," he said. "I heard some of the copilots say if you go manual you can lower the cabin altitude a few hundred feet and the pressure bumps go away."

"Isn't that an emergency procedure?" I said.

"No," he said, "it's working."

I sat back and said nothing. In my vast career as a copilot I always hated the aircraft commanders who would automatically tell me what I was doing was wrong, refusing to listen to another point of view. I wasn't going to be one of those aircraft commanders.

Still, I thought, we were at 35,000 feet and our time of useful consciousness without pressurization would be measured in seconds, not minutes. The manual system required the copilot's finesse on a very small control knob whereas the automatic system was motors, rheostats, and pulleys that removed all human input. The automatic system was used every single flight, the manual system almost never. What can go wrong? What indeed.

The first thing that happened was the air getting sucked out of my chest. Or maybe it was the air crystallizing in front of me into fog. The noise came after. It was a loud roar.

Our pilot oxygen masks were above our heads and I reached for mine instantly, gasping at the cold, sterile air. The next step was to hit a few interphone switches to establish communications with the cockpit crew but that isn't what I did. I reached, cross-cockpit, over the copilot's head to rotate the manual pressure control full clockwise, restoring automatic control.

The air in my lungs returned, the fog subsided, and things were quiet again.

"Don't touch that again," I said to Dellums, "without asking me first."

"Yes," he said meekly, "sir."

Nobody seemed to be injured and some of the passengers in back thought it was fun. Everything was working okay but knowing the manual system wasn't available was worrisome. We descended to a lower altitude, just in case, and landed at our planned destination where I turned the airplane over to the base mechanics.

What they found was the nose outflow valve caked over with tar and nicotine, probably a result of years of smoke exhalations from our communications crews sitting right on top of the thing. The outflow valve, for some reason, was sealed shut until the manual system commanded it full open. They cleaned the valve and cleared us for flight. I spent the flight back to Hawaii conducting a class about the airplane's pressurization system. The more questions I answered, the more confident I became in my systems knowledge.

So, a week later, we had a war story to tell and Lieutenant Dellums had his first "Don't ever touch that" admonition from the old man. He learned that playing around with something in the emergency procedures section of the flight manual is best left for the simulator. Me? I learned that being a crew commander isn't a popularity contest and sometimes you have to squash creativity for the sake of safety.

Rapid Depressurization

Atmospheric Composition & Pressure

[PhysicalGeography.net]
Nitrogen and oxygen are the main components of the atmosphere by volume. Together these two gases make up approximately 99% of the dry atmosphere.

Air is a tangible material substance and as a result has mass. Any object with mass is influenced by the universal force known as gravity. Newton's Law of Universal Gravitation states: any two objects separated in space are attracted to each other by a force proportional to the product of their masses and inversely proportional to the square of the distance between them. On the Earth, gravity can also be expressed as a force of acceleration of about 9.8 meters per second per second.

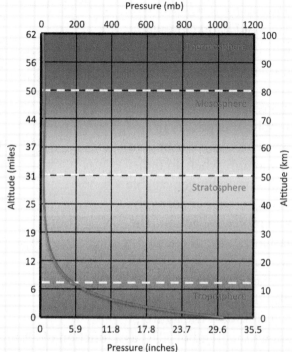

Gravity shapes and influences all atmospheric processes. It causes the density and pressure of air to decrease exponentially as one moves away from the surface of the Earth. [The figure] models the average change in air pressure with height above the Earth's surface. In this graph, air pressure at the surface is illustrated as being approximately 1013 millibars (mb) or 1 kilogram per square centimeter of surface area.

The atmosphere is 79% nitrogen, 21% oxygen, and a bunch of other things in very small quantities. The percentages are pretty much constant with altitude and don't really matter at all . . . what matters is pressure.

By the time you get to 18,000 feet, the atmospheric pressure is one-half what it is at sea level. By 35,000 feet, you are at one-quarter pressure.

Time of Useful Consciousness

[AC 61-107B, ¶2-7.e.(3)] Time of Useful Consciousness (TUC) or Effective Performance Time (EPT). This is the period of time from interruption of the oxygen supply, or exposure to an oxygen-poor environment, to the time when an individual is no longer capable of taking proper corrective and protective action. The faster the rate of ascent, the worse the impairment and the faster it happens. TUC also decreases with increasing altitude. [The figure],

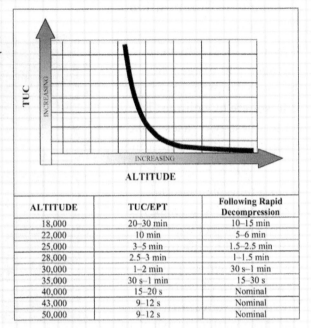

ALTITUDE	TUC/EPT	Following Rapid Decompression
18,000	20–30 min	10–15 min
22,000	10 min	5–6 min
25,000	3–5 min	1.5–2.5 min
28,000	2.5–3 min	1–1.5 min
30,000	1–2 min	30 s–1 min
35,000	30 s–1 min	15–30 s
40,000	15–20 s	Nominal
43,000	9–12 s	Nominal
50,000	9–12 s	Nominal

shows the trend of TUC as a function of altitude. However, slow decompression is as dangerous as or more dangerous than a rapid decompression. By its nature, a rapid decompression commands attention. In contrast, a slow decompression may go unnoticed and the resultant hypoxia may be unrecognized by the pilot.

WARNING: The TUC does not mean the onset of unconsciousness. Impaired performance may be immediate. Prompt use of 100 percent oxygen is critical.

In the early fifties the United States Air Force subjected a group of highly fit, young test pilots to decompression tests in an altitude chamber and came up with what everyone now relies on to determine times of useful consciousness. These times are for an individual at rest, expecting the decompression. Any exercise or fatigue will reduce the time considerably. A rapid decompression can reduce the TUC by up to 50 percent caused by the forced exhalation of the lungs during decompression and the extremely rapid rate of ascent. What's this mean to us? Few of us can expect to last as long as the table would lead us to believe.

The Rules [14 CFR 91.211]

a. General. No person may operate a civil aircraft of U.S. registry—

1. At cabin pressure altitudes above 12,500 feet (MSL) up to and including 14,000 feet (MSL) unless the required minimum flight crew is provided with and uses supplemental oxygen for that part of the flight at those altitudes that is of more than 30 minutes duration;

2. At cabin pressure altitudes above 14,000 feet (MSL) unless the required minimum flight crew is provided with and uses supplemental oxygen during the entire flight time at those altitudes; and

3. At cabin pressure altitudes above 15,000 feet (MSL) unless each occupant of the aircraft is provided with supplemental oxygen.

b. Pressurized cabin aircraft.

1. No person may operate a civil aircraft of U.S. registry with a pressurized cabin—

i. At flight altitudes above flight level 250 unless at least a 10-minute supply of supplemental oxygen, in addition to any oxygen required to satisfy paragraph (a) of this section, is available for each occupant of the aircraft for use in the event that a descent is necessitated by loss of cabin pressurization; and

ii. At flight altitudes above flight level 350 unless one pilot at the controls of the airplane is wearing and using an oxygen mask that is secured and sealed and that either supplies oxygen at all times or automatically supplies oxygen whenever the cabin pressure altitude of the airplane exceeds 14,000 feet (MSL), except that the one pilot need not wear and use an oxygen mask while at or below flight level 410 if there are two pilots at the controls and each pilot has a quick-donning type of oxygen mask that can be placed on the face with one hand from the ready position within 5 seconds, supplying oxygen and properly secured and sealed.

2. Notwithstanding paragraph (b)(1)(ii) of this section, if for any reason at any time it is necessary for one pilot to leave the controls of the aircraft when operating at flight altitudes above flight level 350, the remaining pilot at the controls shall put on and use an oxygen mask until the other pilot has returned to that crewmember's station.

If an aircraft spends more than 30 minutes above 12,500' or any time above 15,000', each occupant must have supplemental oxygen or the aircraft must be pressurized.

Time to Descend

[14 CFR 25, §25.841(a)(2)] The airplane must be designed so that occupants will not be exposed to a cabin pressure altitude that exceeds the following after decompression from any failure condition not shown to be extremely improbable:

i. Twenty-five thousand (25,000) feet for more than 2 minutes; or

ii. Forty thousand (40,000) feet for any duration.

The so-called "4 minute rule" doesn't exist, at least not to say you have to complete the emergency descent in four minutes or less. If you dig deep, however, you can find four minutes as a criteria:

[14 CFR 121, §121.333(e)] When the airplane is operating at flight altitudes above 10,000 feet, the following supply of oxygen must be provided for the use of passenger cabin occupants:

1. When an airplane certificated to operate at flight altitudes up to and including flight level 250, can at any point along the route to be flown, descend safely to a flight altitude of 14,000 feet or less within four minutes, oxygen must be available at the rate prescribed by this part for a 30-minute period for at least 10 percent of the passenger cabin occupants.

2. When an airplane is operated at flight altitudes up to and including flight level 250 and cannot descend safely to a flight altitude of 14,000 feet within four minutes, or when an airplane is operated at flight altitudes above flight level 250, oxygen must be available at the rate prescribed by this part for not less than 10 percent of the passenger cabin occupants for the entire flight after cabin depressurization, at cabin pressure altitudes above 10,000 feet up to and including 14,000 feet and, as applicable, to allow compliance with §121.329(c) (2) and (3), except that there must be not less than a 10-minute supply for the passenger cabin occupants.

It is a technical point here, but just to be clear: under 14 CFR 121, if you don't have enough oxygen on the aircraft for at least 10 percent of the occupants for the times listed, you need to be able to descend to 14,000 feet in four minutes or less. Under 14 CFR 135.157(b) the rule is similar only to 15,000 feet. Part 91? No rule specified.

8: Anticipate

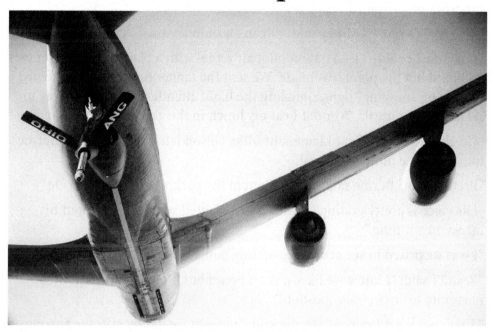

12 ARW KC-135 (USAF Photo)

"We are a little low and a bit right," I said while waving my right hand toward the tanker to get Mikey's attention. "I know pulling back on the yoke will bring us higher, but what else will it do?" He remained quiet in the right seat. "It will cause us to lose a little airspeed. So I need a little more thrust because any extra backpressure is going to cause us to fall back if I don't compensate. If you do things slowly and methodically, you can better anticipate the reactions to your actions." I had to wonder what Bernie Palmer was thinking from the jump seat. I was assigned the trip on Crew Four as Captain Dan Martin was out with kidney stones. Bernie hopped on to give the crew a check ride.

Mikey had asked how to correct elevation without screwing up distance and azimuth, so I asked the tanker for a disconnect to do the demo. We already had our gas and I should have let the tanker go, but this would only take a minute. "Now put your hands around the throttles, Mikey. I'll move the throttles about an eighth of a knob width. The added thrust forces the nose up because our engines are under our wings, so I really don't need any additional pitch pressure. Now we wait." The aircraft appeared stationary for a few seconds until we gradually crept forward and upward. Soon we were at the correct elevation and distance. "Now I take out the thrust I put in and we can work on azimuth."

"That makes sense," Mikey said. "I can't wait to try this."

Of course I couldn't let a new copilot air refuel with a plane full of passengers on board but the point was made. We sent the tanker on its way and turned off the "no smoking" light, signaling the flight attendant that it was okay to serve the next meal. "Mind if I eat my lunch in the galley?" Mikey asked.

"Go ahead," I said. First Lieutenant Mike Gilson left the cockpit and Bernie took his place in the right seat.

"Pretty gutsy," Bernie said, "bailing out of the cockpit on his check ride."

"His voice is pretty grating," I said, "I just wanted some time without his incessant whining."

"I was surprised to see actual instructing going on," Bernie said.

"Yeah," I said, "I know we have pax on board but it seemed like a good opportunity to answer his question."

"That's not what I meant," Bernie said. "I meant we hardly ever see anyone actually explain something like that. Most our instructors believe in 'watch me, now you try it.' Maybe you should be an instructor."

"That will never happen," I said. "Colonel Spindler would never send me to school and I'm not sure I want the two-year commitment. I can get out in just six months."

"You aren't getting out," Bernie said. "You're a lifer."

"So are you," I said, parrying the insult. "I remember when you were a copilot. Look at you now, the chief of standardization and evaluation. That's got to count for something."

"Pilots don't get promoted," Bernie said. "You need something more. I hear they are expanding Walt's office at Pacific Air Forces Headquarters. It's worth considering. Besides, the fun left this squadron when Spindler showed up. He wants to push all of us out."

"Might as well leave," I said. "The airplanes are falling apart and the new generation of pilots are worthless. I just don't know where I want to go."

"You got to figure that out first," Bernie said. "Otherwise you'll never get there."

After we landed at March Air Force Base in Riverside, California, Bernie caught an airliner home and I was left with a few days to ponder my fate while listening to Mikey Gilson complain about the pace of upgrades and the lack of recognition for his obvious skills as a copilot. On the morning of our departure we parked ourselves at base operations to plan the trip home. I checked my flight plan against the navigator's log and realized I hadn't found a single mistake. Captain Mary Marshal was Wrong Way Wong's polar opposite. "Nice log, M-square," I said.

"It was your program," she said. "But if you want to credit me, I'll take any compliment I can get."

I let Mikey fly us home and kept my mouth shut until about three miles on final to runway 8 left at Honolulu. The instrument landing system was down for maintenance but the weather was CAVU, ceiling and visibility unlimited. Mikey pushed the nose over once we were cleared for the visual approach and we soon found ourselves just a few hundred feet over the Pearl Harbor channel. "You better hope there are no aircraft carriers heading out to sea," I said. "We need to be higher."

"Nah," he said, "I think we are okay." I let him continue and was surprised when he chopped the power at 50 feet despite our shallow approach. As we fell earthward I resisted the urge to take over, thinking it would be bad, but not too bad. We touched down hard about halfway into the runway overrun, bounced, and settled onto the runway.

"A shallow approach," I said, "requires more power for longer. It is very hard to judge."

"You should have told me that sooner," Mikey said. The next week my mailbox had the usual post trip critique from the passengers and my landing was topic one on the list of complaints.

The second piece of paper in my mailbox was a set of orders to instructor pilot school. Most of my peers either politicked endlessly to be selected, or traveled in the woodwork to avoid it. I had done neither. Staring at me, from the bottom of the form, were two empty check boxes above a line for my signature. "Accept" or "Decline," the choice was mine.

I thought about my options on the way home, thinking I wasn't ready to get out of the Air Force but I wasn't really looking forward to staying in. The *Lovely Mrs. Haskel* fixated on one word and one word only: "instructor."

"You were meant for this," she said. "You think of yourself as an engineer,

Eddie. But you aren't." She let the words hang as we sat in my home office. With a four bedroom house and no kids, we had rooms to spare and the largest of these was filled with aviation books and homemade computer gear. "You spend all those hours soldering gizmos and cursing at computer code. You are happiest when you are teaching, you need to do this."

I signed the orders and a month later signed into the Strategic Air Command's instructor school. The Air Force Boeing 707 community (the EC-135, RC-135, and WC-135 squadrons) was not large enough to warrant an instructor school so we went to the KC-135 tanker instructor course. We were not responsible for aircraft specific knowledge, only for the art and science of instructing pilots.

"You have to learn how to talk and fly at the same time," the course's senior instructor said on day one. "Jet fuel isn't cheap and you have to impart maximum knowledge in minimum time, all while flying the airplane with an unqualified block of clay sitting in the other seat."

On sortie one my unqualified block of clay was KC-135A instructor pilot Major Bob LaFrance. He was doing his best to be the world's worst copilot upgrading to pilot. "When you get to the perch," I said as he flew the airplane on a downwind leg about 2 miles from the runway, "you will need a gentle 25 degrees of bank and can begin your descent."

Bob gently rolled the aircraft right and pushed the nose down with enough force to throw me against my shoulder straps. We lost five hundred feet of altitude in a second. "I've got the airplane," I said. "Bob, we don't need to lose all our altitude at once. Let's try being a little more gradual."

"Okay," he said, grinning. He managed to roll out on an extended centerline and land the airplane exactly where it needed to be. I pushed the throttles forward and moved the flap handle from its landing to its takeoff setting. Bob drifted left of runway centerline. "Need to come right," I said, "do it now." Bob smashed in a healthy amount of rudder and I was treated to a view of the grass on the opposite side of the runway.

"I've got it," I said, correcting to centerline. "I'll get us back on downwind, Bob." I rotated the airplane, raised the landing gear, called tower with our intentions, and rolled into the crosswind turn. "Bob," I said, "let's talk about keeping the airplane on centerline."

"How do I do that?" he asked. I spoke at length while flying the airplane and looking outside for conflicting traffic. I forced my eyes inside for a moment only to be greeted by the altimeter blasting through our traffic pattern altitude. I shoved the nose down. "Is that how we level off?" Bob said in his faux dummy voice. I looked at him and could not suppress a laugh.

Bob maintained the idiot pilot persona until we walked into the training center debrief room. "You should sit down and come up with a script," he said, "several scripts. But you should know ahead of time the quickest way to get your point across while flying the airplane. And make sure you give your student measurable things to do. Don't 'say lower the nose,' say by how much. Don't say 'correct left,' say 'a little left rudder.' You've got to make every word count."

I sat down that night with a pad of paper and started to draw. A visual pattern took between 6 and 10 minutes, leaving very little time to instruct. Most of the instructors at the 9th ACCS didn't do a lot of talking in a visual pattern, but none of our pilots were of Bob LaFrance's mock ineptitude. But they were close. Our squadron was getting younger and we were no longer able to hire the top of the volunteer list, we would get whomever the Air Force decided to send. The days of having a Bernie Palmer or Jon Patrick show up at our door were over. From here on out, we would be teaching

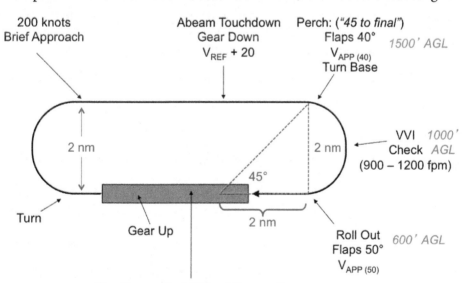

Instructor's B-707 visual pattern lesson plan (Eddie's notes)

guys like Mikey Gilson. I would need these instructing skills, no doubt about it.

The next day, I handed the airplane over to block of clay LaFrance after leveling on the downwind leg. "You had the bank angle just right yesterday," I said, "so let's add altitude control on base to your skills. How far do you want to lower your nose on base, Bob?"

"About 5 or 10 degrees," he said. "Or maybe 10 or 15."

"Let's try 3," I said. "We are 1500 feet above the runway right now and we want to roll out at 600 feet, so we need to lose 900 feet. We can check our progress halfway around the turn."

Bob did as instructed and we found ourselves halfway around the turn at 800 feet. "We are just a little low," I said, "but much better than yesterday. So how should we adjust our pitch now, Bob?"

"A little less?" he said.

"Very good." Bob did great and as the program continued I started to suspect he was trying more to demonstrate his superior airmanship than his acting skills. The school included ten flights, but most of those were for the tanker pilots. I found myself finished with the program on sortie three. I was given the next seven sorties to watch other instructor students flail. That ended up being the best instruction of all.

Visual Approach

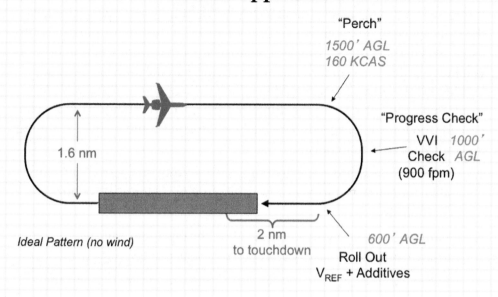

The "ideal" depends on airplane and pilot. Using a G450 as an example, the airplane starts the base turn at 160 knots and rolls out precisely on final at 600' AGL and 2 nautical miles:

- Starts with a downwind displaced 1.6 nm from the runway at 1,500' AGL.

- Begins the base turn at the "perch," which is abeam your desired 2 nm roll out point.

- Rolls smoothly into a constant 25° of bank and allows the nose to drop into a 900 fpm rate of descent.

- With half the turn completed, half the altitude to lose is lost so the airplane is about 1,000' AGL.

- Rolls out at 600' AGL on an extended centerline, 2 nm from the desired touchdown point, setting up a stabilized approach.

- The 1,500' AGL starting point seems to be an international standard for jet aircraft, the 25° of bank is an industry norm for transport category aircraft, and the 2 nm extended final is what is needed to provide a 3° stabilized approach.

Downwind (Drift)

It is important to have the aircraft in trim, on altitude, and flying parallel to the runway when on downwind. This will give you the opportunity to establish a level flight power setting and to judge any crosswind drift. But how do you judge drift? The standard method of flying parallel to the runway and looking for the ground track in front of you moving left or right may work in a Cessna 150 but it is not the thing to do in a jet. You shouldn't fixate your gaze for too long at jet speeds, especially when you should be busy scanning for traffic. Three better choices:

1. If your compass card has a drift indicator, simply turn to roll out so the course indicator (set to the runway heading or reciprocal) is under the drift indicator.

2. If your avionics provides a drift reading, fly a heading adjusted to compensate from the runway heading's reciprocal, corrected for drift.

3. You can compute drift using a circular computer given TAS and the crosswind.

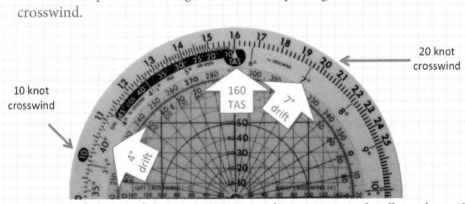

For example: if you are flying 160 KTAS a 10 knot crosswind will produce 4° of drift and a 20 knot crosswind will produce 7° of drift.

Downwind (Displacement)

Your displacement (no wind) should equal at least twice your turn radius. The turn radius for a standard rate turn completed at less than 170 knots can be estimated by dividing your TAS in nm/min by 3. Example: flying the base turn at 150 knots is 2.5 nm/min, which divided by 3 equals a 0.83 nm turn radius. Doubling that means your diameter is 1.67 nm.

The "Perch"

We often speak of the point to begin the base turn as described by a 45° line from our touchdown point. This military method of defining the "perch" does not work in a modern environment where we want to have a stabilized final approach no later than 500' AGL. As a technique, we use a 2 nm final approach. The 45° line would work for an airplane with a 2 nm downwind displacement. For our example aircraft, we will have to fly about a half mile beyond the 45° line.

Base Turn Adjustments - Up to 15 knots of wind

This technique allows us to roll out on course if we adjust our bank angle by the drift angle prior to the turn. Since our target bank is 25° and we cannot exceed 30° under most circumstances, we will use 5° drift as our limiting correction. When flying at 160 KTAS it takes 15 knots of crosswind to generate 5° of drift so that is the limit of this technique. To adjust:

- Take note of the drift angle on downwind. Your avionics may provide the number for you or you may have to take note of the heading required to maintain a parallel downwind.

- If the wind on downwind is pushing you to the runway, it is an overshooting wind. If you steepen your base turn bank angle by the drift angle, up to 30° of bank, you should roll out on extended centerline.

- If the wind on downwind is pushing you away from the runway, it is an undershooting wind. If you shallow your base turn angle by the drift angle, to as little as 20° of bank, you should roll out on extended centerline.

Base Turn Adjustments - Over 15 knots of wind

If you have a severe undershooting wind, roll out 90° to the runway on base, begin your turn to final when a 25° bank turn will place you on the extended centerline.

If you have a severe overshooting wind, you should widen your pattern as much as allowed to stay in protected airspace. If the winds are too strong to allow this, you might consider the winds will exceed your crosswind landing limits.

Rolling Out on Extended Centerline

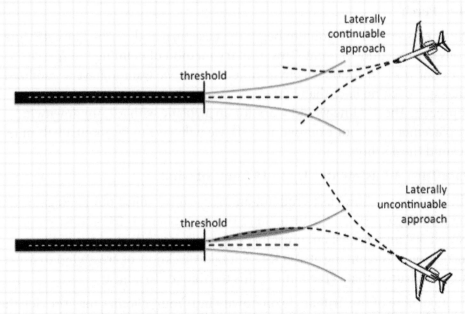

There is more art than science when it comes to judging the roll out, but there are ways to help yourself.

- ILS or Localizer (best option)
- Synthetic Vision (another very good option)
- LPV ("localizer performance" but some aircraft may struggle to display the course if the turn in is made too close to the runway)
- VOR, NDB (acceptable, provided they are aligned with the runway)
- RNAV, GPS (acceptable, keeping in mind the centerline of the course might not precisely align with the runway)

9: An Instructor's Notebook

C-141 (USAF Photo)

As an aircraft commander my days were consumed with getting the squadron's very first personal computer up and running and ironing out the bugs in my fuel computation, navigation, and takeoff data programs. Of course I flew a Westpac trip every five weeks and was treated to a local training sortie two or three times a month. As an instructor pilot, I anticipated my days would be consumed with flying and teaching.

"What's this?" I asked when handed a twenty-page message from the Pentagon.

"It's a new way of doing procedure turns," Major Condit said. "You learn it and teach the rest of us."

An Air Force C-141 crew was violated in South Africa for using U.S. procedures when entering a procedure turn at Kruger Mpumalanga Airport. They were flying the procedure precisely as required by Air Force Manual 51-37, Instrument Procedures. These procedures were in complete agreement with the U.S. Federal Aviation Administration but in complete disagreement with the International Civil Aviation Organization, the ICAO.

We had been taught that every procedure turn in the world could be entered using the same procedures as called for by a holding pattern. We were taught wrong. As I dove into the message I felt angry that I had flown over much of the world without this knowledge, but intimidated by having to replace a one-paragraph procedure with pages of instructions I did not understand. It was a mess that started with their entry into what the ICAO calls a course reversal.

The crew was headed southeast toward the Kruger Mpumulanga non-directional beacon (NDB) with clearance to fly the approach and to contact the tower once inbound.

They were heading 140°, about 90° from the inbound course. Our instrument manual said:

"A parallel procedure turn entry may be used any time. If the inbound procedure turn course is within 70° of the aircraft heading, turn outbound toward the maneuvering side to parallel the inbound procedure turn course. If the inbound procedure turn course is not within 70° of the aircraft heading, turn outbound in the shorter direction to parallel or intercept the inbound course."

The aircraft was not heading within 70° of the inbound course, so the crew turned right to parallel the procedure turn course. It was just as the book told them.

There was no radar cover-

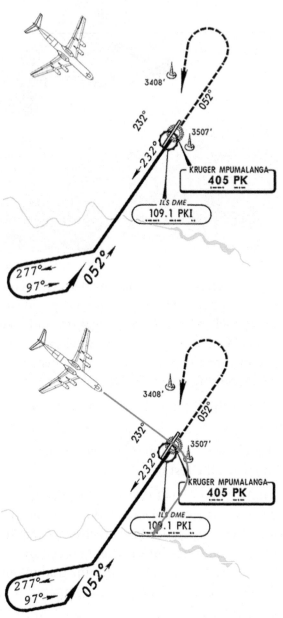

age but when tower realized what they had done the crew was violated because they overflew noise sensitive areas just east of the course. How would a left turn have been any better?

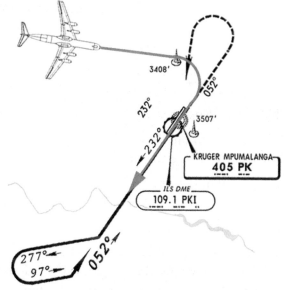

ICAO Document 8168, Volume 1, Section 4, Paragraph 3.3.1 has this to say on the subject:

"Unless the procedure specifies particular entry restrictions, reversal procedures shall be entered from a track within ±30° of the outbound track of the reversal procedure. However, for base turns, where the ±30° direct entry sector does not include the reciprocal of the inbound track, the entry sector is expanded to include it."

The crew should have asked for maneuvering airspace north of the NDB so as to arrive within the 30-degree sector.

The concepts were difficult because they changed with each type of approach. We no longer had a one-size fits all entry procedure. These ICAO procedures worked in the United States, but U.S. procedures did not always work when flying internationally. I drew up an instruction manual of my own. The squadron resolutely rejected the manual. "Too complicated!"

I sat down the day prior to my next training sortie with our newest aircraft commander, Captain Jeffery Preston, and Lieutenant Jon Patrick, to cover the procedures in detail. I drew pictures on a chalkboard and we "chair flew" each entry. As I instructed the procedures began to solidify. We each took a turn at flying a course reversal the next day and with the help of a one-page cheat sheet, we managed to fly the ICAO way.

Each time I repeated the "instruct, chair-fly, airplane-fly routine," the new and strange procedures became easier and easier. After a month I had the procedures down cold and most of the squadron's pilots at least understood how to enter an ICAO course reversal. Only Lieutenant Colonel Spindler refused to learn. "I'll always have one of you peons by my side."

Course Reversals (ICAO)

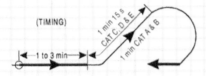 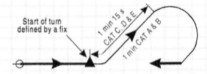

45° / 180° Procedure Turn

[ICAO Document 8168, Vol 1 §4, ¶3.2.2.3 a] 45°/180° procedure turn starts at a facility or fix and consists of:

1. a straight leg with track guidance. This straight leg may be timed or may be limited by a radial or DME distance;

2. a 45° turn;

3. a straight leg without track guidance. This straight leg is timed. 1 minute from the start of the turn (Category A and B aircraft); 1 minute 15 seconds from the start of the turn (Category C, D and E aircraft); and

4. a 180° turn in the opposite direction to intercept the inbound track.

The 45°/180° procedure turn is an alternative to the 80°/260° procedure turn unless specifically excluded.

Unlike the U.S. FAA Standard Procedure Turn, also known as the 45°/180° Procedure Turn, the straight leg without track guidance is timed under ICAO procedures. The timing is mandatory unless a DME limit is given.

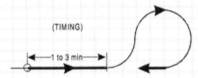 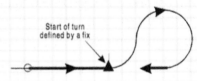

80° / 260° Procedure Turn

[ICAO Document 8168, Vol 1 §4, ¶3.2.2.3 b] 80°/260° procedure turn starts at a facility or fix and consists of:

1. a straight leg with track guidance. This straight leg may be timed or may be limited by a radial or DME distance;

2. an 80° turn;

3. a 260° turn in the opposite direction to intercept the inbound track.

The 80°/260° procedure turn is an alternative to the 45°/180° procedure turn unless specifically excluded.

The only advantage of the 80°/260 over the 45°/180° is time: it gets you pointed back to the runway more quickly. But there is a big disadvantage: adjusting for wind, the only correction available to you is bank angle. If the wind is strong enough, you could find yourself blown onto the non-protected side before completing your turn inbound. ICAO says "the 45°/180° procedure turn is an alternative to the 80°/260° procedure turn unless specifically excluded," you would be wise to use the 45°/180° if there is any kind of wind.

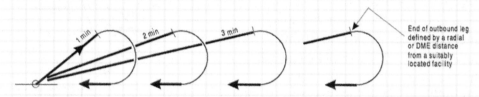

End of outbound leg
defined by a radial
or DME distance
from a suitably
located facility

Base Turn

[ICAO Document 8168, Vol 1 §4, ¶3.2.2.3 c] Base turn consists of:

1. a specified outbound track and timing or DME distance from a facility; followed by

2. a turn to intercept the inbound track

The outbound track and/or the timing may be different for the various categories of aircraft. Where this is done, separate procedures are published.

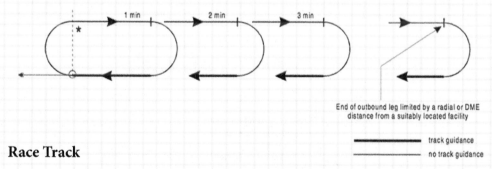

End of outbound leg limited by a radial or DME
distance from a suitably located facility

⎯⎯⎯⎯⎯⎯ track guidance
⎯⎯⎯⎯⎯⎯ no track guidance

Race Track

[ICAO Document 8168, Vol 1 §4, ¶3.2.3] A racetrack procedure consists of:

1. a turn from the inbound track through 180° from overhead the facility or fix on to the outbound track, for 1, 2 or 3 minutes; followed by

2. a 180° turn in the same direction to return to the inbound track.

As an alternative to timing, the outbound leg may be limited by a DME distance or intersecting radial/bearing.

45°/180°, 80°/260°, and Race Track Entry Procedures

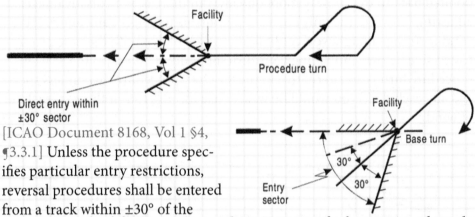

Direct entry within
±30° sector

[ICAO Document 8168, Vol 1 §4,
¶3.3.1] Unless the procedure specifies particular entry restrictions,
reversal procedures shall be entered
from a track within ±30° of the
outbound track of the reversal procedure. However, for base turns, where the
±30° direct entry sector does not include the reciprocal of the inbound track,
the entry sector is expanded to include it.

You've got to be within these entry sectors to be permitted to begin the
45°/180°, 80°/260°, or base turn procedure. What if you aren't?

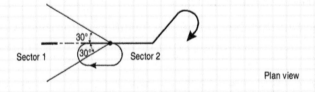

Plan view

Sector 1: Arrivals from this sector may enter
the reversal procedure directly

Sector 2: Arrivals from this sector must enter the
holding prior to the reversal procedure

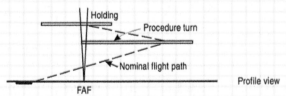

Profile view

Most of these procedures have a holding pattern nearby and ICAO Document 8168, Vol 1, figure I-4-3-4, states "arrivals from this sector must enter
the holding prior to the reversal procedure." What if there isn't a holding
pattern depicted? I would request "maneuvering airspace" opposite the
course reversal so that I could maneuvering the aircraft into the entry sector.

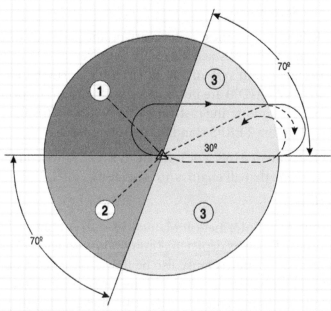

[ICAO Document 8168, Vol 1 §4, ¶3.2.3.2]

Normally a racetrack procedure is used when aircraft arrive overhead the fix from various directions. In these cases, aircraft are expected to enter the procedure in a manner similar to that prescribed for a holding procedure entry with the following considerations:

1. offset entry from Sector 2 shall limit the time on the 30° offset track to 1 min 30 s, after which the pilot is expected to turn to a heading parallel to the outbound track for the remainder of the outbound time. If the outbound time is only 1 min, the time on the 30° offset track shall be 1 min also;

2. parallel entry shall not return directly to the facility without first intercepting the inbound track when proceeding to the final segment of the approach procedure; and

3. all manoeuvring shall be done in so far as possible on the manoeuvring side of the inbound track.

Non-Emergency Statement

U.S. FAA. [TERPS ¶ 200.b.] These criteria are predicated on normal aircraft operations for considering obstacle clearance requirements. Normal aircraft operation means all aircraft systems are functioning normally, all required navigational aids (NAVAID's) are performing within flight inspection parameters, and the pilot is conducting instrument operations utilizing instrument procedures based on the TERPS standard to provide ROC.

ICAO. [ICAO Document 8168, Vol 1 §2, ch. 1, ¶1.1.2] Procedures contained in PANS-OPS assume that all engines are operating.

Wind Corrections

U.S. FAA [Aeronautical Information Manual §5-4-9] A hold-in-lieu of procedure turn must be flown as depicted. Though not explicitly explained, the 45°/180* and 80°/260° patterns must also be flown as depicted but the point at which the turn may be commenced and the rate of turn is left to the discretion of the pilot so long as the remain within distance is adhered to.

ICAO. [ICAO Document 8168, Vol 1 §2, ch. 1, ¶1.1.3] All procedures depict tracks. Pilots should attempt to maintain the track by applying corrections to heading for known wind.

10: Spindler's Gambit

Shemya (USAF Photo)

"Shemya," the scheduler said, "you and Condit." I was listed as the aircraft commander but Major Condit was senior. I knocked on his office door and he gestured me in.

"You been to Shemya before?" he asked.

"No, sir."

"Me either. There's a rule about Shemya: you can't go unless you been. Well, no pilot in this squadron has ever been there so we are stuck. It will be you and I next week. I'm too busy to find out what all the fuss is about, so you do the leg work and I'll watch you fly."

"Yes, sir."

He handed me a manila folder with typical trip information: crew names, passenger data, and itinerary. It was my flight crew minus copilot Dellums, who was on the mainland on vacation. The communications and maintenance team were familiar too. I didn't recognize half the security team. In back would be one of our regular teams of Navy passengers probably on some kind of inspection of support facilities for their nuclear submarine fleet. Shemya, I knew, was a postage stamp-sized island in the Aleutian Island chain halfway between Alaska and Russia. It was host to an Air Force Base with a reconnaissance unit and some kind of clandestine eavesdropping unit aimed toward the Russian skies.

There had been a crash of an RC-135 there a few years back so I called the Pacific Air Forces headquarters safety office who confirmed they had the report on file. I was just about out of the squadron and thought I might avoid detection while passing the commander's office, but it wasn't meant to be.

"Captain Haskel," Lieutenant Colonel Spindler said.

"Yes sir," I said.

"Come on in, have a seat." I entered the office of pain and regret, wondering why the normally foreboding colonel was wearing a warm smile in place of his usual sneer. "Congratulations," he said. "I heard from the schoolhouse that you did very well."

"I learned a lot," I said.

"Good," he said. "This puts you into a new league, Eddie."

It was the first time he had ever addressed me by my first name. He spoke at length of the responsibilities of being an instructor pilot and how I would have new opportunities thrown my way. "You have to seize opportunities, Eddie. Sometimes you won't recognize them, but remember you have to seize them."

"I will seize them," I said.

With that, he dismissed me. I left the squadron parking lot thinking either Spindler had a personality transplant in the last month or was playing some kind of game. I was so consumed with the paranoia that I missed my turn to the Pacific Air Forces building and had to double back. Once there, I was presented with a green folder marked "CONFIDENTIAL" and labeled with an ink stamp and handwritten entries:

15 MAR 81, RC-135, 61-2664, 6 fatalities, PAEI – PASY

The airplane was flying on its routine mission to position its crews from their home base, Eielson Air Force Base near Fairbanks, to their deployed location on Shemya Island. The weather was awful, but not bad enough to cause a crash and the loss of 6 crewmembers. The survival story was fascinating. The airplane impacted a hill just short of the runway where anti-tank stanchions left over from World War II remained. They tore the airplane apart and hindered rescue efforts. I had to remind myself I wasn't looking for crash survival hints, but crash avoidance clues.

After an hour of study I came to the same conclusion the Air Force Accident Investigation Board arrived at three years ago. The copilot flew the approach below the radar controller's glide slope intentionally as part of a misunderstanding of the approach procedure. That placed him and the aircraft in an unrecoverable position late in the approach when either a shift in wind direction or speed pushed the airplane further below glide path and right into the hillside. It was exactly as I had been taught at safety school: most aircraft losses are caused by pilots flying perfectly good aircraft into the ground.

The only kind of approach available at Shemya was a PAR, "Precision Approach Radar." It was the standard instrument approach many years ago, but now it was relegated to the military at obscure locations too remote to have a modern instrument landing system. A radar controller painted the aircraft on a scope and gave the pilot headings and descent cues. The headings were straightforward: turn left 300 degrees, right 305 degrees, and so on. The descent information was a bit trickier: begin descent, you are on glide path, you are slightly above glide path, you are below glide path, you are well below glide path, and so on.

The worst thing you could hear was "you are too low for safe approach, go around." That could be the last thing you ever hear. I think I heard that once in the simulator but never in an airplane. We routinely flew these with the landing gear up, the flaps at 30 degrees, and at an intermediate speed. When the controller said, "begin descent" we would extend the landing gear and the remainder of the flaps, lower the nose a few degrees and watch the vertical velocity indicator drop to 700 feet per minute rate of descent. TLAR: "That looks about right." From there on it was a game of adjustment. If you were slightly low, you added a few percent of thrust and increased the pitch a half a degree. TARA: "That Ain't Right, Adjust."

The next day I called airline pilot Kevin Davies, who was a Shemya pro from his days in the C-141. "The weather never changes at Shemya," he said. "You'll have a 300 foot ceiling, 30 to 35 degrees Fahrenheit, and a stiff crosswind of 25 knots. But the PAR controllers are the best in the business."

Then I called the 6th Reconnaissance Squadron at Eielson Air Force Base. I found out their RC-135s had a lot in common with our EC-135s: same engines, same wing, and about the same weight. That's also when I learned about their "point of no return" ritual.

The point of no return means different things to different aviators, but at

Shemya it was all about divert fuel. Our aircraft's maximum landing weight was generally around 200,000 pounds. With a typical load of passengers that usually meant we couldn't land with much more than 40,000 pounds of fuel. That wasn't enough to miss the approach at Shemya and return to the nearest runway long enough to handle us. So until you decided the weather was good enough, you had to keep enough fuel on the airplane to make it to your alternate. At that point you dumped the excess fuel overboard and you were committed to land at Shemya.

The flight from Honolulu to Shemya is just over 6 hours after you throw in a holding pattern at low altitude just east of the island. The winds were generally from the west but on any given day could be from any direction. We were treated to a 30-knot headwind which meant our equal time point favored Hawaii. If, for some reason, we needed to put the airplane on the ground as soon as possible, the equal time point told us which alternate was closer. After 3 hours and 10 minutes we knew our closest destination was Alaska.

Major Condit was as good as his word and played his role as the world's most overpriced copilot. Everything was going smoothly. We planned one orbit to gauge the weather and another to dump our extra fuel. We would need 40,000 pounds of fuel to make it to Anchorage plus another 10,000 for reserve. With today's passenger load, our maximum landing weight would permit only 35,000 pounds of fuel. We had sixty thousand on board.

"Shemya weather," the radar controller announced, "is one mile, two-fifty overcast, temperature one degree, dew point zero, winds are three-one-zero at forty gusting to fifty."

Major Condit fumbled with our squadron in-flight guide. He was looking for the crosswind chart. "That's twenty-five," I said. "A thirty degree cross comes to one-half the component." He was undeterred and continued his task.

"Well captain," he said as if it was just a routine report, "you've got a twenty-five knot cross and everything else is just in limits. Whatcha wanna do?"

"Commence fuel dump," I said, "ask for the PAR, start the approach checklist."

I heard the click-click of the interphone system, denoting our hot microphone system in the cockpit was now tied to the rest of the airplane, inviting passengers and crew to listen in on our approach. It was a silly annoyance I could have done without, but that's the way we did things. I could hear the faint rumble of the hydraulically driven fuel pumps in the body of the aircraft running to push twenty-five thousand pounds of fuel, almost four thousand gallons, into the cold Aleutian air.

The PAR controller greeted us and gave us the usual preliminaries, including "no need to acknowledge transmissions." He would be talking to us continuously and we would need to listen closely. Finally he said, "approaching glide path, wheels should be down." I gave Major Condit a thumbs up and inverted my hand to point downward, his signal to extend the landing gear. Our cockpit routine would be with hand signals only during this part of the approach. As the rumble of the air announced our transition I asked for the final notch of flaps. I allowed the landing gear's drag to overwhelm the changing camber of the wing and held the pressure on the yoke steady. Our VVI, the vertical velocity indicator, crept down to 700 feet per minute, right where I wanted it. "On course," the controller said, "going slightly below glide path."

It shouldn't have been, everything was right out of the textbook so far. When in doubt, I knew, do nothing. "On course, going further below glide path."

Well now I had a problem. The VVI was right at 700, the airspeed was steady, I hadn't moved the throttles since leaving the holding pattern. "Nav, what's our ground speed?"

"Rawgh," Wong said.

"One-oh-five," Condit said.

A hundred and five knots? Our approach speed was 147 knots. I pulled the nose up slightly and added a quarter of a knob-width of power on the two inboard engines.

"Turn right two-nine-five," the controller directed, "now slightly left of course and holding below glide path. Adjust your rate of descent."

Now this was bad. Not only was I low, now I was moving off course and the controller was starting to tell me how to fly the airplane.

"Tighten it up, Eddie." Now Major Condit was concerned.

Fifty knots of wind from thirty degrees off runway heading meant a twenty-five knot crosswind. A fifteen-degree correction to course made sense. I banked slightly into and out of the turn to watch the heading bug settle on 295. Fifty knots of wind from thirty degrees off runway heading also meant a heck of a lot of headwind. The cosine of 30 is one-half, that's how I knew the crosswind component without looking it up. What is the sine of 30? Just over point eight? That would make it a 42 or 43-knot headwind. That's why 700 fpm was too much! In pilot training our first jet, the T-37, made its approaches at right around 100-knots. The VVI in that thing was usually about 500.

I raised the pitch further and brought the outboard throttles to match the inboards. The VVI crept up to 200. "Turn left two-nine-zero, correcting to course, correcting to glide path." I pulled the outboards back an eighth, relaxed some backpressure, and pulled the inboards to match the outboards.

"On course, on glideslope."

At 300 feet Condit said "nothing so far," and then, "oh, it's to the left. The runway is to your left."

I looked up and sure enough, the runway was to our left. The strong crosswind meant our nose was a good 20 degrees upwind to maintain course and our first glimpse of it would be to our left. I slid a healthy dose of left rudder and right aileron and landed the aircraft.

We had the next three days off with not much to do. The base wasn't set up for tourists and didn't want to spend any extra effort to entertain us. Our passengers, I am sure, got the royal treatment. All this ended for me on day two when a pilot from the RC-135 unit approached me at the base operations building.

"You Captain Haskel?" the lieutenant colonel asked. "You the pilot on that silver and white bird?"

"Yes, sir."

The colonel introduced himself as the detachment commander and invited the crew for a tour of the island. Nobody else was interested so I agreed to go solo.

The RC-135, my host explained, was known as the Cobra Ball. They flew airborne reconnaissance of Russian test missile shots just a few hours east of Shemya. The big radar on the end of the island, Cobra Dane, did the same thing from the ground. Somewhere off the island was a ship known as Cobra Judy. We finished the tour with a look inside the Cobra Ball, an ugly monster of an airplane with all sorts of stuff strapped to its right side for reasons I wasn't permitted to know. The colonel invited me to sit in the pilot's seat where I got the nickel tour. It was much like our own aircraft, with a few extra navigation computers thrown in and about half the communications equipment I was used to. It was a good way to waste a day, but I had had enough.

"I noticed an air refueling receptacle on your airplane," the colonel said before I could climb out of the seat, "are you receiver qualified?" I told him I was. "Instructor?" Yes again. The questions continued: how many hours, what was your commission date, how many years on station in Hawaii, any promotion pass overs, and finally, "How would you like to fly the best mission in the Air Force?"

"Thank you for the offer, sir," I said. "But I am a brand new instructor pilot and would like to spend at least a year with my unit to polish those skills."

"You can polish your skills up here," he said. "Besides, I have your commander's endorsement. He volunteered you for the job. Colonel Spindler called our headquarters in Fairbanks. I think you will be seeing orders very soon. Welcome aboard."

Major Condit denied any knowledge of the ruse that just played out for my benefit, but he did confess that Spindler had been plotting my exodus for months. "I was surprised as anyone when he sent you to instructor school," Condit said. "I wasn't sure about the end game, but I guess now we know."

When we got back I found my orders waiting for me but this time without "Accept" or "Decline" check boxes. "The orders are printed," Lieutenant Colonel Spindler said, "your only option is to accept them or to put in your papers to separate from the Air Force. Either way is fine with me, you will cease to be my problem."

"When in doubt," the saying goes, "do nothing." I left the orders to Alaska in my mailbox, as if unread. Maybe they would just go away if I ignored them long enough.

Equal Time Points (ETPs) and Point of Safe Return (PSR)

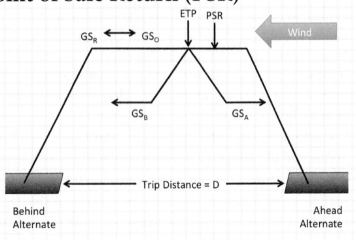

Most texts talk about departure and destination airports when considering ETPs when in fact your ETP airports are normally the closest available either side of the ocean or remote area you are crossing.

$$\text{Ground Distance to ETP} = \frac{(D)\,(GS_B)}{GS_A + GS_B}$$

Where:

D = Distance between behind and ahead airports

GS_A = Ground speed going to ahead airport

GS_B = Ground speed going to behind airport

Note: the ground speeds are considering loss of engine, altitude, etc. so that the equal time point becomes the decision point for which alternate to choose in the event of a problem. Typically three are computed: (1) Loss of one engine, (2) Loss of pressurization, and (3) all engines operating.

$$\text{Ground Distance to PSR} = \frac{(\text{Endurance})\,(GS_R)\,(GS_O)}{GS_O + GS_R}$$

Where:

Endurance = Total fuel quantity / Average Fuel Flow

GS_R = Ground speed returning to departure airport

GS_O = Ground speed outbound

Note: unlike the ETP alternate airports, the PSR airport is normally the original departure airport, since that is where you are likely to return.

11: Number Crunch

Hilo Airport, left base (Courtesy of photographer Breanna Anderson)

"Fly right along the west edge of the bay," I said from the right seat as Bernie played the dummy pilot in the left. "You want to roll out a mile and a half from the end of the runway. The coast here is two miles from the runway so that gives you a half mile to make the turn."

"Is that enough?" Bernie asked.

"I think so," I said. "A half mile turn radius for pattern speeds rings a bell."

"I'm pretty sure that is right," Bernie said. "But don't quote me on it."

As check rides go, Bernie gave more than his share of busts but this one went well. We grew up as copilots together and now we were starting to feel our oats as the senior cadre in the squadron. "You going to Alaska?" Bernie asked.

"I don't know," I said. "I was hoping some higher power would intervene."

"You might get your wish," he said. "There were two crashes in Japan last week, and Pacific Air Forces Headquarters is going ballistic. I heard they are going to put a freeze on all instructor pilots and force a certain kind of instructor into becoming instrument specialists."

"What kind of instructor is a certain kind of instructor?" I asked. "And how do you know all this headquarters gossip?"

"Certain instructor pilots," he said, "are better at math than others. You know what I'm talking about." That was true, pilots with engineering degrees used to be common but in our generation they had become few and far between.

"And where did you hear all this?"

"Let's just say I'm not going to be in the squadron forever," he said. Bernie was never open about his intentions. I always thought I was his best friend in the squadron, but he did spend a lot of time with Walt.

The next week the assignment freeze was official and my orders to Alaska were cancelled. A letter from the headquarters general informed every pilot in his command that all pilots had to become instrument pilot experts and every base must have at least one expert trained at the Air Force Instrument Instructor's Course. All assignments would be contingent upon having such a pilot remaining on base.

"Get ready for some more schooling," Walt said on the phone. "The safety office up here just put out a priority request for a replacement safety officer to free you up for the instrument instructor's course."

"Why me?" I asked.

"Because the last two guys from Hawaii washed out," he said. "They have strict orders that every base send somebody who can pass and they figure any engineer has a better chance of meeting the math requirement. Colonel Spindler has zero credibility up here and they aren't even going to ask him. The orders are being cut."

The next week we were informed that an EC-135 pilot from our sister squadron in Oklahoma was on his way to become our new safety officer and I was headed back to school.

My class was twenty-five senior pilots, those with the star on their wings that denoted seven years of Air Force pilot history, and two of us with less experience. The two of us with "slick wings" were also the only non-fighter pilots. The other "heavy driver" was from a fighter base flying combat C-130s and seemed more at home with them than with me. The instructor introduced himself as Captain Bob Duncan, "but you can call me Big Dick." There was some laughter. "I can't help it that I have a big dick," he said, " but some peo-ple call me "Footer." That was enough evidence for me to place Footer in the fighter pilot category.

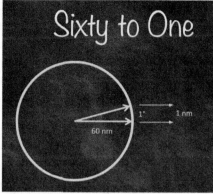

He pulled a chalkboard on wheels to the center of the classroom and drew a circle with two arrows from the center to the circumference. The arrows were 60 nautical miles long and appeared to form a triangle with a base of 1 nautical mile. "If anyone can explain this to me right now," Big Dick said, "I will give you credit for the course and you can go home today."

Nobody else ventured an answer so I thought "why not?" Without raising my hand I said "Sixty times the sine of 1 degree equals 1. Give or take."

"You know that for a fact?" Big Dick asked.

"No," I admitted, "it's just a guess."

"Well no credit for guesses," he said, "but it was a damned good guess. You are right." There was some snickering from the back of the class, answering my "why not?" question. The instructor went on to explain the unifying theory for all aviation mathematics. If Einstein was a pilot, he would have approved.

Big Dick explained the distance of an arc along a circle is equal to the sine of the angle describing the arc times the radius of the arc. In the case of our 60 nm radius and 1° arc:

Arc Distance = 60 nm x sin (1°) = 1.047144 nm

"If an engineer is looking for the answer one and gets the answer one point oh four seven one four four, what does he call that?" The instructor was look-ing right at me.

I preferred to remain in the woodwork in these classes, but I had already violated that rule. "Deviation," I said.

"And what does a pilot call it?" Big Dick was now looking to the rest of the class, which was keeping quiet. "A real pilot calls it bullshit," the instructor answered his own question. "Can you read zero point oh four seven one four four on any instrument? Of course not! If your calculations are off by zero point oh four seven one four four do you give a shit?" There was some laughter. "Of course not. For the purposes of our math, it's close enough! Is that okay with you mister engineer?" He was looking at me. I nodded meekly, reminding myself to never again be the first to answer in class. "Good," the instructor said, "so that's step one in our path to sixty-to-one nirvana. Let's take the next step, my young apprentices."

With a quick swipe of an eraser and some chalk, we had a new board to look at. This one I couldn't explain and fortunately Big Dick had tired of making sport of me in front of the class. (He actually bought me a beer that night at the bar, saying I was the first student to ever answer his opening question correctly.) His explanation was arithmetic genius.

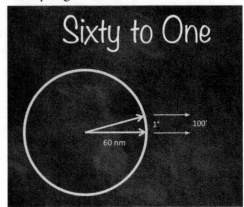

We had already seen proof that 1 degree of arc and 60 nm of radius comes to 1 nautical mile. And we all knew a nautical mile equals 6,076

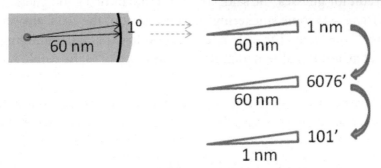

feet. It was just simple multiplication and division. You replace the 1 nm with 6,076' (they are the same thing, after all). If you divide 60 nm by 60 and 6,076' by 60 you haven't changed the shape of the triangle. And the rest is mathematical magic.

"Let's call it 100 feet," he said, "because 1 foot is . . ."

"Bullshit!" all of the class said, finishing his statement.

"Good," he said, "and a hundred feet equals a flight level."

"Here it is boys and girls," he said to our all male class, "the crux of this class, the foundation of everything you will ever do as an instrument pilot. If it was up to me, we would tattoo these words on every pilot's forehead in reverse, so he would wake up every morning and have to stare at them in the mirror while shaving. The smarter among you will realize that means you should be writing this down."

He gave us example after example and I raced to keep up with my pocket calculator doing the math the old fashion way, with trigonometry. It all worked brilliantly.

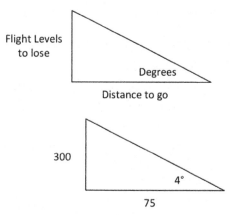

Let's say you are at 35,000 feet, 100 miles out and must level off at 5,000 feet by 25 miles. You have to lose 300 flight levels in 75 miles, 300 divided by 75 is 4 degrees.

We did a lot of mental math and, as every engineer knows, you can't do real world math without including the units. We stopped talking about velocity and either spoke of "nautical miles per hour," "nautical miles per minute," or whatever the situation dictated.

"Wouldn't it be a handy thing to know," Big Dick asked, "exactly what VVI you want when descending on a non-precision approach?"

This was precisely what I wanted. My efforts to date produced pages on pages of tables, one for each approach we flew. Nothing I did was worthy of mental math. I had tried, but more times than not I would confuse myself and revert to "dive and drive" rather than underestimate the descent needed.

"Well feast your eyes on this," he said, looking straight at me. It was, to over use the word of the class, brilliant.

His equation said we could simply multiply our ground-speed (in nautical miles per minute) by our descent angle and come up with the vertical velocity (VVI) needed to

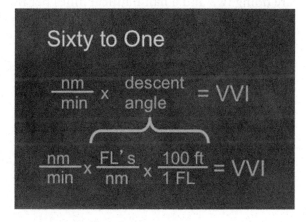

make the descent. What kind of witchcraft was this?

We had already proven that descent angle is equal to flight levels to lose divided by nautical miles to lose. Multiplying by 100 feet and dividing by 1 flight level was the same as multiplying by one; it just made the units agree. So here, at long last, was an easy way to figure vertical velocity on a non-precision approach:

Nautical miles per minute times descent angle times 100 gives vertical velocity in feet per minute.

For the next three weeks we were treated to revelation after revelation about how instrument flight can be more precise. "Death to TLAR," became our mantra. "That Looks About Right" certainly works in aviation, given enough experience and luck. Sixty-to-One, on the other hand, eliminated both requirements and allowed all instrument pilots to fly with greater precision.

I came back to the squadron with a stack of formulas, rules of thumb, and an evangelical zeal to teach.

With every flight, as I tried to pass on my newfound knowledge, the concepts became solidified and every instrument approach became a predictable, repeatable event. Most of my students reacted with polite appreciation, but few seemed to grasp the mathematical beauty of it all. It took someone I really trusted to bring me back to earth.

"Right now we are flying 150 knots true airspeed," I said to Bernie as we repeated our visual pattern at Hilo from a few months back. "I know my turn radius will be equal to our nautical miles per minute divided by three. We are doing two and a half nautical miles per minute. Two point five divided by three is zero point eight. So we need more than the half mile we talked about last time."

"Okay," he said, "about a mile. Don't confuse things with math, Eddie."

60 to 1 (Engineer to Pilot Translation)

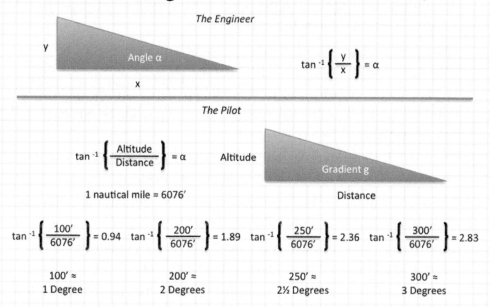

At Air Force Advanced Instrument Instructors School they taught everything in instrument flight can be traced back to the 60 to 1 relationship: what happens when you divide just about everything by 60.

To an engineer this is demonstrably false in most cases. The true explanation happens with the trigonometric function called the "tangent" which is based on the relationship of the angles inside a triangle with the legs opposite and adjacent to those angles. The "arctangent," often written $\tan^{-1}$, produces the angle given these sides.

Does a pilot care about any of this? No, not really. So the Air Force Advanced Instrument Instructors School solution is to turn the math that we don't care about into a few of their rules of thumb that make flying airplanes more precise and easier, which is to say, safer:

- Arc around a point. To fly an arc around a point, use a bank angle equal to the turn radius times 30 divided by the arc radius.

- Arc distance. The distance traveled along an arc is equal to the arc radius times the arc angle divided by ten.

- Descent gradient. Flight levels divided by nautical miles to lose equals the descent gradient. Nautical miles per minute times descent angle times 100 gives vertical velocity in feet per minute.

- Glide path on final. Nautical miles per hour times ten divided by two gives a good three degree glide path VVI.

- Holding pattern teardrop angle. A holding pattern teardrop angle of 120 times the turn radius divided by leg length will provide an on course roll out, no wind.

- Top of 3 ° descent. Start descent at three times your altitude to lose in thousands of feet to achieve a three degree gradient.

- Top of a 2.5° descent. Start descent at four times your altitude to lose in thousands of feet to achieve a 2.5 degree gradient.

- Turn radius (standard rate). A standard rate turn is possible up to 170 knots TAS and has radius is equal to nm/min divided by 3.

- Turn radius (25° bank). A 25° bank angle turn will be needed above 170 knots TAS and has radius equal to (nm/min)² divided by 9.

- Visual Descent Point. A Visual Descent Point is found by subtracting the touchdown zone from the Minimum Descent Altitude and dividing the result by 300. (For example, let's say the MDA is at 1000' MSL and the touchdown zone elevation (TDZE) is at 250' MSL. Your VDP would be at (1000 - 250) / 300 = 2.5 nm. You need to start down from the MDA when 2.5 nm from the end of the runway.

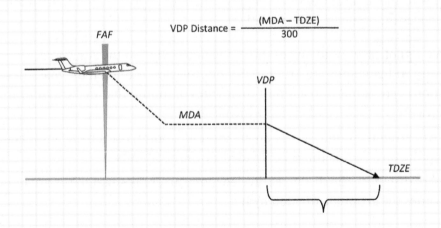

12: Asymmetric

EC-135 62-3579 Ellsworth (TSGT Michael H. Haggerty, USAF photo)

"I'm too busy," I told the scheduler. "Any run of the mill aircraft commander can fly this."

"You are the only one available," he said. "A day to airline to Dallas and a day to fly her home. Two days, easy."

Few aircraft commanders volunteered for these because it was a big headache. The airplane was never ready on time after months of maintenance and something was sure to go wrong. This particular airplane had been under heavy maintenance for over a year. The depot decided the maintenance did not merit a test flight so we would be the first crew to take the craft airborne in all that time.

The copilot and navigator spent the week prior on the mainland before making their ways to Dallas. I found them in a bar within crawling distance of the hotel and got ready for step one in my campaign to soften my hard ass image: chit chat like a normal crew dog.

"So here he is," Mikey said, "a navigator's best friend." Mary blushed.

"I was meaning to ask you about that," I said.

"It's your navigation program," she said. "We are the only unit in the big airplane Air Force that has one. Everyone in the ACCS world knows about it. We got it. They don't."

"So navigators don't have to worry about mission planning," Mikey said, "and copilot's don't have to worry about fuel logs. Maybe you are my best friend too."

"Computers are making us all lazy," I said.

"Here's to laziness," Mikey said, raising his beer.

"Here, here!" Mary said.

The banter between Mikey and Mary was tempting, but worry got the better of me and I returned to my room after a single beer. I studied the charts and looked for every divert airport within 200 miles of our route from Dallas to Honolulu. It may have been due diligence or outright paranoia, but the thought of flying that airplane thousands of miles after sixteen months of maintenance unnerved me. The airplane was ready on time the next morning.

"Takeoff checklist," I ordered from the left seat as I steered the airplane onto Love Field's westerly runway. Mikey switched what needed to be switched, and toggled what needed to be toggled. "Takeoff checklist complete."

I pushed the four throttles to their approximate maximum rated thrust positions and lightly held my hand above while Mikey fined tuned each lever from below. "Power set."

The airplane accelerated smoothly and the speed shot up quickly past 100 knots. We used a series of speeds as decision points and the first was "S-1," the point at which we could lose an engine and continue the takeoff or abort the attempt and stop on the runway remaining. Either action would require we do everything just right, but engines almost never fail at precisely that speed. If the engine failed prior to that speed, we would abort. The lower our speed, the easier that would be to do. If the engine failed above that speed we would continue. The more speed we had, the easier that would be.

"S-1," I heard over the interphone from the right seat and then "number two is rolling back," and then "no oil pressure on two," and then "there goes two."

I pushed a little right rudder to keep the airplane straight on the runway and glanced at the airspeed indicator. We still had twenty knots until I could rotate but we still had almost half the runway in front of us. Not too bad.

"Rotate," Mikey called as that magical speed came.

As the airplane left the runway and the altimeter started to climb I saw Mikey reach down for his checklist. "Gear up," I said, "you can get to that later." He lowered the checklist and raised the gear handle. I stole a look at the engine instruments. The needles on the remaining three engines were not parallel. Two of the oil pressures did not agree with the third and there was a mismatch in fuel flows.

"Throttle for failed engine," I said as if reading it from the checklist, "cut off." Mikey, I am guarding one, three, and four. Pull the number two throttle over its detent.

"Fire switch isn't needed," I said. "Trip the generator." Mikey did so.

"Flaps up," I said, "declare an emergency and tell them we want an immediate landing at Carswell."

Mikey made the call and I turned the airplane a few degrees to the right to set up for a left base turn to the Carswell Air Force Base north-south runway.

"We should get to a holding pattern," Mikey said, "so we can catch up on these checklists."

"Do you know why the engine failed?" I asked.

"No," he said, "but we haven't run the engine failure, after takeoff, climb, descent, or approach checklists."

"The only checklist you need," I said, "is the before landing checklist. I don't know why the engine failed. But after these guys have been working on them for a year, I am worried about the other three."

Mikey grumbled, as he often did, but complied. "I think this is a mistake," he said as I turned the airplane to align with Carswell's runway. "We should hold," he said as I ordered he extend the landing gear and another notch of flaps.

As the gear indicators switched from UP to DOWN and the red light in the gear handle extinguished, Mikey pointed at the engine instruments. "The fuel flow on number one is way high," he said. "Maybe we should land."

"Good idea," I said. "Full flaps." At about five hundred feet I glanced around the cockpit and everything seemed to be in order. We landed. Carswell Air Force Base is home to B-52s with the same engines as ours and they provided a team of mechanics that made quick work of the troubleshooting.

"You guys are lucky you didn't lose all four," the lead mechanic said. "The oil reservoir caps on all four engines were never torqued down and they were all bleeding oil right out of their cowls. The fuel lines on number one and two were just finger tight. In another ten minutes you would have been down to two engines."

They promised to have us running in a few hours. Mary and Mikey found two quiet rooms at base operations and raced each other to sleep. I wandered the halls for a bit and when I returned to the flight planning room I found another crew in the middle of their briefing. The aircraft commander was a skinny captain of average height. His copilot and the navigator were lieutenant colonels. The flight engineer was a master sergeant. I wondered what kind of crew rates such horsepower? And how does a mere captain get command of such an august crew?

Their flight suit patch revealed the logo of the 1st Airborne Command Control Squadron, the big kahunas in our ACCS world. They flew Boeing 747s on a classified mission none of us on the outside were privy to. As they briefed I tried to busy myself without being obvious. While rereading the crew notices for the Eastern Pacific for the third time I heard my name.

"Are you Captain Haskel?" The 747 aircraft commander asked.

"Yeah," I said, "I'm Eddie."

"I'm Steve," he said. "The line crew were talking about you landing that EC-135 with only one engine. Said you didn't even break a sweat."

"Not even close," I said. "We had one engine shut down and were about to lose a few others, but we got her on the pavement before it got too bad."

Captain Kowalski said he had flown for our sister squadron, the 7th ACCS, when he got the call to fly the Boeing 747. "With the airlines hiring we aren't getting the normal flow of highly experienced majors with walk-on-water-records like we used to. The last guy we hired busted his check ride with United Airlines so we are hiring again."

"United?" I asked.

"Yeah," he said. "The Air Force doesn't have a schoolhouse for 747 pilots, so we contract that out to the airlines. Thing is we have to pass an airline transport rating flight evaluation and not everyone does."

We spoke for a few minutes, trading EC-135 stories when he finally asked the question I was waiting for. "Are you receiver qualified?" Yes. "You an instructor?" Yes. "You ever bust a check ride?" No. "Do you have at least 2,500 hours total flight time?"

"Well no," I said. "I'm still shy of 2,000 hours."

"Oh," he said. "Well, it never hurts to volunteer. You want to interview? The squadron commander is on the airplane right now."

I followed Captain Kowalski outside and was treated to the prettiest airplane I had ever seen. When you've grown up flying small fighters and trainers, a Boeing 707 seems large. But even after spending five years on the 707, nothing prepares you for the first time you walk right up to a 747. Just as nobody can truly really appreciate the Grand Canyon from a photo, nothing compares to the mass and beauty of the seven four up close. Armed guards with serious faces and serious weapons surrounded the aircraft.

"We are testing the airplane's ground power systems and brought her here for a few hours," Kowalski said. "We don't have any passengers or a communications crew today but the airplane doesn't go anywhere without the guards." I followed him up a set of airstairs, up another set of stairs to the main deck, and then up the spiral staircase that became a signature of the airplane from its earliest days. Sitting at a table in the upper rest behind the cockpit was Lieutenant Colonel Don Ellison.

Steve introduced us and we talked for about 30 minutes. He wanted to know about my landing with three engines on fire and all hell breaking loose. Of course I had to correct the tall tale.

"You are pretty modest for a pilot," he said. "We usually hire guys with bigger egos."

"I'll learn to fake it, sir."

"Well you work on those hours and maybe we'll give you a call someday."

A day later we were back on Oahu where the southern sky quite often had a Boeing 747 landing or taking off at Honolulu International. I could never look at them again without a wistful thought of the airplane of my dreams.

The day after the assignment freeze on all instructor pilots was lifted, the base got a new wing commander who announced all his division chiefs would be field grade officers, officers of the rank major or higher. "Captain Palmer's done a great job," Colonel Wayne said at our next squadron meeting, "and we are going to reward him with a kick upstairs." Bernie had orders to join the Pacific Air Forces Headquarters staff with Walt.

After the wing commander left, Lieutenant Colonel Spindler introduced our new chief of standardization and evaluation. "Major Leonard Jones hails from our sister squadron in England and comes highly recommended. Would you like to say something, Lenny?"

The major confidently strode to the front of the room. He was a slight man, perhaps five-foot-five at best. His salt and pepper hair betrayed a younger face. He forced a smile to offset the scowling words to follow.

"There's a new sheriff in town," he said. "I've heard you've had it easy out here in the Pacific. Well all that ends now." With that, he looked to Lieutenant Colonel Spindler who nodded his approval. After the meeting, most of the pilots huddled in a worried scrum.

"Who is this asshole?" Dan Martin asked.

"I heard from one of the radio operators he got into trouble in England," Jon Patrick said. "He scared his passengers half to death overbanking the airplane on a visual approach and they refused to ever get on an airplane with him again. The squadron there was looking to get rid of him just as our squadron was looking for a major." Jon was the Crew One copilot and would be working directly for Major Jones.

"I don't normally like spreading unsubstantiated rumors," I said. "But any one willing to alienate every pilot in the squadron on day one probably deserves it." The crowd drew silent and all heads turned to the door behind me. I turned my head to see Major Jones.

"We all get what we deserve," he said. "Colonel Spindler gave me specific instructions to weed out the troublemakers. It will be a pleasure to bust you, Haskel, the first chance I get." He let his words hang waiting for a comeback. I kept my mouth shut. He turned to face Jon. "Captain Patrick, let's go."

Jon Patrick got up to leave behind Jones. After they both departed, Jon peered back and grasped his neck with both hands, as if choking.

The only hurdle between Major Jones and his seat of tyrannical power was a local check ride. Bernie asked me to fly in the jump seat as an extra pair of eyes. I managed to keep my silence until air refueling. Jones was required to demonstrate the limits of the air-refueling envelope by methodically flying from the center to the limits of each axis, in turn.

"Twenty-two up," the boom operator said. At this point we would expect Jones to spend ten seconds to point out visual references and then to return to the center of the elevation envelope at 30 degrees, but that's not what he did. He moved left. "Eight left, twenty-two up," the boom operator said.

"Major Jones," I said, "we don't allow the limits to be combined, it isn't necessary and it risks breaking something."

"You guys are pussies," Jones said. "This is how we did it in England." He started edging forward. The boom operator fired the disconnect circuit.

"Return to pre-contact," the boom operator ordered.

"Is there a problem?" Jones asked.

"Unlike you active duty types," a different voice said over the radio, "we like to take care of our equipment in the Air National Guard. If you don't want to play by the rules we'll take our business elsewhere."

"Okay," Jones said. "We're done then." With that he slammed the throttles shut and we fell away from the tanker, thirty minutes early. Bernie looked at me and shook his head. We had planned on rotating the seats so all three pilots could get some air-refueling time but now that plan was for naught.

We headed to Barbers Point Naval Air Station, just a few miles west of Honolulu. The check ride would require a mix of four-engine and three-engine instrument approaches, landings, and an engine failure simulated at 200 feet above the runway after takeoff.

Each approach was adequate, not bad enough to fail him but really not up to our standards. Bernie would have lots to critique. The touch and go landing was a bit longer than we liked but certainly not terrible. After each takeoff I noticed that Jones skewed his head slightly, trying to anticipate the moment Bernie would pull either the number one or number four throttle to simulate the engine failure.

Many multi-engine pilots treat the engine failure after takeoff as a manhood test to see how quickly they can apply corrective rudder. After a series of fatalities in large Air Force aircraft, our squadron began preaching doing the maneuver deliberately and slowly. Applying the wrong rudder slowly was recoverable; doing so quickly could flip the airplane upside-down in seconds.

I saw Bernie brace his left leg, telling me he was going to pull the number four engine. The correct response to a failed right engine would be to press the left rudder to compensate for the excess thrust on the left. If the student were to press the wrong rudder, in this case the right rudder, the instructor would feel the wrong rudder pedal move aft in his feet and should be able to stop it before it became critical. His hand hovered over the number one throttle, an extra bit of theatrics he refused to give up. As soon as the altimeter passed 200 feet he pulled the number four throttle to idle. I saw the blur of Jones' right leg stomp on the right rudder.

In an instant the airplane was nearly inverted. "I've got it, I've got it! Get off the rudder!" Bernie was yelling at the top of his lungs and managed to wrestle the airplane right side up, "Get out of the seat, Eddie take over."

Jones jumped out, grinning from ear to ear as if he had just flown the perfect check ride. I hopped in and got us back to Honolulu. Bernie sat quietly in the right seat. I negotiated with Honolulu tower for an immediate landing and in fifteen minutes the nightmare was over. Well, my nightmare was over; Bernie's continued. I sat in the squadron ready room, straining to decipher the raised voices behind the squadron commander's closed door. After an hour Bernie came out and the door closed behind him.

"Buy me a beer?" Bernie asked. It would be the first time I ever saw him drink. We adjourned to the golf course bar where, after his first beer and halfway into the second the details emerged.

"I busted him," Bernie said. "Colonel Spindler said I couldn't do that. When I told him I already reported the results to Pacific Air Forces headquarters he went ballistic. He called headquarters and they said only I could change it. He handed me the phone and I told them it was a clear-cut bust; I had to take control to prevent losing the airplane. They agreed. I handed the phone back to Spindler and he started yelling at them until they hung up on him. Major Condit tried to calm him down but when he reminded him that the squadron still needed a new chief of stan/eval, Spindler started yelling at Condit. That's when I left."

After his third beer Bernie became philosophical and realized that in a week it would no longer be his problem. He would be a staff officer at headquarters and somebody else would have to deal with it.

For the next few days I replayed the flight in my mind, over and over again. We were rolling rapidly through 90 degrees of bank before Bernie reversed the rudder and brought the number four throttle back to full power. The bank angle stabilized around 130 or so until the number four engine spooled up and pushed the right wing upward until we were right-side-up. I was convinced the airplane could fly with an outboard engine out and no rudder at all.

The next week Bernie got his wish for a training flight with just me at his side. I watched from the right seat as he completed what would be his last takeoff, his last receiver air refueling, and then the traffic pattern at Kahului Airport on Maui. "Can we try something new?" I asked.

"You promise not to scare me?" he said.

"This is going to be the tamest engine failure you've ever experienced," I said. "When we get to 200 feet after takeoff, I want you to put both feet on the floor. Do not press either rudder. I am going to pull the number four throttle and I am going to tell you when I do it. All I want you to do is keep the wings level with ailerons. If you don't like the way the airplane is flying, you can add rudder, add power, do whatever you need to do. But as long as you think we are flying okay, try it my way."

Bernie agreed, but he reminded me of my promise not to scare him. I asked tower for permission to fly north four or five miles before turning downwind and they agreed. After his touch and go I began. "Feet on the floor," I said. "I'm pulling the number four engine now." As the thrust decayed to zero the left wing started to rise, the two engines on the left overpowering the one engine on the right. "Keep the wings level with ailerons only," I said. Bernie moved the yoke to the left and our wings were level. "We are flying, Bernie. We have an engine out, no rudder, and we are flying. Sure we are flying a little sideways, but the airplane is safely flying. There was no need to react quickly. Quick risks death; slow and methodical, that's the way to go."

"Nobody is going to like this," Bernie said. "You need to keep the airplane coordinated or you aren't going to climb as fast as possible."

"That's right," I said. "So look at your hands. Which one is lower?"

"My left," he said.

"Step on your low hand," I said. He fed in left rudder and the airplane was flying straight again.

"You need to teach every instructor this," he said.

For the next month I did just that and the reaction was split. Major Condit was impressed and promised to use it as his standard demo. "Too many pilots think getting the rudder in as soon as any yaw is detected is a macho test. But how can anyone really detect that kind of yaw with any kind of turbulence or wind gust pushing the nose around. This is going to save lives, Eddie."

"Stupidest thing I ever heard of," Lieutenant Colonel Spindler said. "We've never done it this way and we aren't going to start now. Besides, your days as an instructor are over."

He didn't explain and I didn't figure it out until we got back to the scheduling office. My name was moved from Crew Five to Crew One. I looked at the scheduler, who shrugged his shoulders. "We can't find any EC-135 instructor pilots above the rank of captain in the entire United States Air Force?" I asked.

"There's a catch," the scheduler said. "The Pacific Air Forces Headquarters rule for a chief of standardization and evaluation requires a clean record. No busts, no pass overs, no drunk driving record. There aren't many of those."

The next day I was to report to headquarters for evaluator pilot training.

Asymmetric Thrust

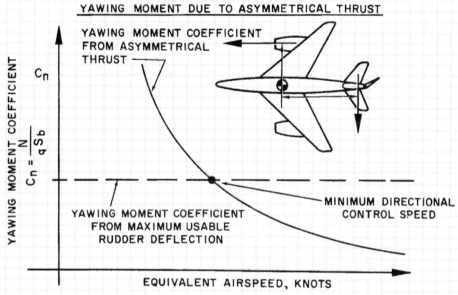

YAWING MOMENT DUE TO ASYMMETRICAL THRUST

[Air Training Command Manual 51-3, pg. 294.]

The design of a multiengine airplane must account for the possibility of an engine failure at low airspeed. The unbalance of thrust from a condition of unsymmetrical power produces a yawing moment dependent upon the thrust unbalance and the lever arm of the force. The deflection of the rudder will create a side force on the tail and contribute a yawing moment to balance the yawing moment due to the unbalance of thrust.

Your rudder was designed to handle this, there is no reason to worry that it won't. As long as you've only lost one engine and you get the correct rudder in smoothly, you should be able to handle any speed the engines will give you with the rudder you have.

Due to the side force on the vertical tail, a slight bank is necessary to prevent turning flight at zero sideslip. The inoperative engine will be raised and the inclined wing lift will provide a [component] of force to balance the side force on the tail.

Our entire emphasis is getting the correct rudder. We don't want to apply rudder in the wrong direction and we don't want to have rapid rudder reversals.

Note: What follows is all technique. It works in every Boeing and every Gulfstream I've ever flown but I recommend you try it out in the simulator to make sure it will work for you.

Issue One: Rate of Recognition

You are probably wondering why "rate of recognition" is more important than direction; it is getting the wrong rudder that will kill you, after all. And that is why the rate of recognition is more important. Rate as in "not too fast." We used to teach engine failures after takeoff by requiring the student to keep both feet planted on the floor and forbade the use of rudder until the direction puzzle was solved. We would delay this to the point the aircraft is flown for ten or fifteen seconds with no rudder correction at all. Guess what? Most airplanes fly just fine with an engine out at traffic pattern weights.

Issue Two: Direction

You suspect that getting the wrong rudder can kill you and in many airplanes it can. So before you even think about pressing either rudder pedal, do this:

1. Look at the attitude indicator and look for roll. (Yes, roll, not yaw.)

2. Correct the roll with ailerons only. (Just level the wings.)

3. Look at the yoke: which side is lower? That's the side you've added aileron because the good engines are on that side trying to roll you into the dead engine.

4. Verify the slip indicator agrees with your hands, it will be deflected to the good engines.

5. You will be needing to add rudder where your low hand and slip indicator are pointed. "Step on the low hand, step on the ball."

Issue Three: Rate of Rudder Application

You took your time getting here so there's no rush in actually getting the rudder in. Press half of what you think you need and wait. If you need more, add more. But it is important to apply the rudder in one direction and try to minimize rudder reversals.

13: An Examiner's Notebook

Crew One: Kenny, Haskel, Giffords, Patrick (Eddie's Collection)

Having spent the first six years of my Air Force career getting an average of four check rides a year, I thought running a standardization and evaluation program had to be the easiest job in a squadron. I would have the best schedule, nobody would critique my flying, and I could be mean to anyone of my choosing for any reason without fear of retaliation. All of that turned out to be exactly true. But that was only half the job.

I had a regular crew of four from the flight deck, a flight attendant, and six from the various communications specialties. Each was a flight examiner. Dealing with those who worked for me was easy. It was those I worked for that posed the challenge.

Every flying squadron is a political organism with births (new people in), deaths (old people out), and lots of growth (upgrades). There is pressure within from the crewmembers getting check rides, from the training instructors trying to push students through the system, and from the outside.

"Your guys busted three radio operators in a row," Lieutenant Colonel Spindler said with his ever-present scowl. "You need to exercise some control over your people, captain."

"You can't turn these people loose without more training, sir. If these young kids can't do their jobs unsupervised, we shouldn't qualify them."

"The next time I get a complaint from the Navy," he said, "I'm telling them we don't have enough crews because of a chief of standardization too drunk on power to keep the big picture in mind."

The big picture. I thought about that a lot. Captain Carl Giffords was worried one of our navigators would lose the big picture somewhere between Hawaii and Japan. Left unsaid was that navigator would have a record with Carl's signature of approval. "She meets standards," he said after giving Captain Mary Marshall her annual evaluation. "But she's lazy and only does the bare minimum. You would tear her apart if she were on your crew."

"If she meets standards and you are still uncomfortable," I said, "then maybe the standard is too low."

"It is," he said. "But the squadron has to agree to a higher standard and they won't. Besides, you are partly to blame."

"Me?"

"Yeah, you." He said. "Those computer programs turned hours of mission planning into minutes. Most navigators don't put in the time to get familiar with the flight anymore. I hear the same thing about the copilots. We are getting lazy as a squadron and need to tighten up the training programs."

The complaints were similar in every crew position. As the chief of standardization, it fell upon me to lobby the chief of training to improve the training and to convince the squadron commander to raise the standards. But I had done my best to alienate them both.

"You need to spend less time showing off behind the tanker," I told Major Jones behind closed doors, "and more time getting your copilots proficient so they can pass an upgrade check ride."

"How much instructing have you ever done?" he asked, knowing the answer wasn't much. "You should spend less time bad mouthing me and more time instructing when you get the chance. And if you are going to bad mouth me to my face, I expect you to add the word 'sir' before, and, or after each sentence."

My only hope was to outlive Spindler and Jones. But I was on my third reprieve, and the next assignment down the system was likely to take. The squadron was on a hiring binge of experienced pilots, all Spindler allies.

"You are booked for a check ride tomorrow," the scheduler said. "Major Compton is getting his aircraft commander qualification check."

"Compton?" I asked. "Never heard of him."

"He just arrived."

I picked up his grade folder and read. Major Richard Compton was an EC-135C pilot from the 2nd Airborne Command Control Squadron, the guys who fly the "Looking Glass" mission. The 2nd ACCS had an airplane airborne continuously since the early sixties and their pilots flew a lot. Major Compton's record was filled with over 10,000 flight hours. Compared to my 2,000 hours, Compton ought to be good.

As he settled in behind the tanker I noticed an economy of motion. His left hand moved only when the tanker's bank changed and his right hand barely moved at all. The airplane rarely moved more than a degree up, down, left or right. Our check ride grades were given as "Unsatisfactory," "Satisfactory," and "Exceptional." After giving check rides for more than a year, I had never given an unsatisfactory or an exceptional. It looked like he might have the first "E" awarded to a squadron pilot in over two years.

As we departed the air-refueling track I asked for and was cleared directly to a holding pattern just north of Kona, Hawaii. Our inertial navigation system drew a line directly to the fix. Major Compton pulled out the approach plate and studied, while motioning a right turn with his hands. "We are heading 080 degrees, the inbound course is 174 degrees, we are outside the 70 degree entry cone, and so we are going to make a left turn entry to parallel the outbound course." True enough, I thought. But why make this call at 25,000 feet when the winds are bound to be different on the approach at a lower altitude?

As we descended, Major Compton talked incessantly. "After we turn inbound I will be asking for flaps thirty. Once the glide slope begins to move I'll ask for the gear." He never asked for my opinion, and this being a check ride, I never offered one. Not that I would have a chance; he just wouldn't stop talking. Passing 10,000 feet the wind direction changed and our heading to the holding fix moved to the right. I turned in my seat and looked at the navigator. "You got anything to say?" I asked.

"No, sir." Captain Mary Marshall didn't owe me a "sir," but that was par for the course on a check ride. I was hoping to exonerate her from what I thought was on the horizon. It appeared she didn't want my absolution.

As we got to the holding fix our heading was 120, only 54 degrees from the inbound course. The rules said turn right and our turn radius would make a left turn unacceptably wide. As the inertials counted down to zero, Compton banked left.

"I've got the airplane," I said. Compton let go of the yoke and I reversed the bank. "We'll talk about this on the ground, Major Compton. Don't let it bother you, just fly the holding pattern from the right and continue to fly as well as you have been. You've got the airplane."

"Okay," he said. "I've got the airplane." He flew the remainder of the holding pattern within standards and his first few approaches were very nice.

After half an hour at Kona we popped over to the east side of the Big Island and flew an arc approach into Hilo. The approach started with an arc of ten miles radius around Hilo VOR for about a half of a circle. We required our pilots keep within a half-mile of the arc for a passing grade and they could do that with a constant bank angle or by bracketing the arc with a series of straight legs. Most pilots bracketed the approach by flying with the needle pointing between 10 degrees above the inside wing tip and 5 degrees below.

"I haven't done this since pilot training," Compton said. "Hardly seems fair."

"I suppose," I said. "Just give it your best shot." Compton dipped his left wing for about 5 degrees of bank and watched the distance of the arc shrink from 10 nautical miles to 9.5. He took out the bank and once we got back to 10 nautical miles banked again, this time with about 3 degrees. From that point, the distance never varied by more than 0.1 nautical miles. "The best I've ever seen," I said. "Well done."

Compton had all his requirements met except for a four-engine landing back at Honolulu. He flew us back to Oahu, chatting with the navigator whenever he spotted something new. "And what's that poking out of the clouds over there?" he asked.

"Maui," she said. "It has some kind of Hawaiian name."

"Haleakalā," I said. "It is the house of the sun." They chatted easily as I contemplated my near future. If Compton flew the rest of the check ride without incident, the holding pattern would just be a few minutes of critique and a valuable lesson in keeping aware of the changing conditions with altitude and location. 'You can't prejudge the winds,' I would say, and everyone would nod in agreement because I would have spared them a busted check ride. A "career defining moment," some call these busts. But if something else happened, I would have to document the holding pattern and if I did that, I would have to bust the navigator too. That would make a messy situation even worse.

Major Compton went from his easy banter back to the hyper play-by-play once we turned inbound on the approach back at Honolulu. He intercepted the instrument landing system perfectly, centered each needle, and nailed the airspeed all the way through glide slope intercept, still talking. When he flew this type of approach with three engines back at Kona, he extended the landing gear when the glide slope started its move from the top of the case and the rest of the flaps once it had centered. Not this time.

As we started our perfect 700 feet per minute descent, the speed started to pick up. "We are looking for 136 knots at this weight," he said, "that usually takes around 1400 pounds per hour per engine but that is only approximate. Today it is only taking 1100, not a big deal."

Perhaps that should have clued him, maybe not. Flying down the glide slope at most weights with the landing gear and final flap setting increased the drag of the airplane and the thrust requirement. Having the engines at a higher thrust setting was desirable since it reduced the spool up time in the event of a go around. The cockpit was unusually quiet. That was another clue unnoticed. But I couldn't blame him for missing that; he was too busy talking to listen to the airplane. The rulebook said the gear had to be down no later than glide slope intercept or the final approach fix. We were past both. I picked an altitude.

At 1,000 feet I announced over the interphone, "Major Compton, I am extending the landing gear and I'll get you the rest of the flaps."

"Thanks," he said.

As we walked back into the squadron Major Compton turned left into the squadron commander's office and I headed for a phone. "How'd it go?" I heard as I passed the office.

"Not too bad," Compton said. "No check ride is perfect but I think I did pretty good, boss. Haskel said my arc was the best he had ever seen!"

I wasn't required to pre-brief the squadron commander but given our already strained relationship I thought it best. "I have to fail Major Compton and Captain Marshall both," I said as he sat, speechless. "I have two safety of flight busts and don't have a choice in the matter."

"We'll see about this," Spindler said. "You don't just take out a major and the squadron's best navigator just because you don't like them. You have a lot to learn about life outside the cockpit, Haskel. You are about to get a lesson about how the real world works. Dismissed."

I submitted the check ride paperwork, answered one phone call from headquarters, and another from the scheduler. With Major Compton busted, the squadron was suddenly down a pilot and I would have to take the trips he had been scheduled to fly.

Maintaining an Arc

Bracket Method:

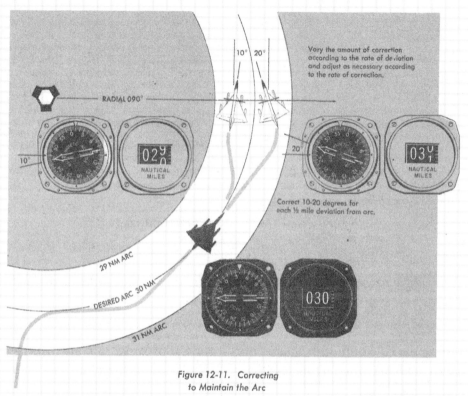

Figure 12-11. Correcting
to Maintain the Arc

[AFM 51-37, pg. 12-8] Under no-wind conditions, the aircraft will fly in an exact circle around the station by maintaining a relative bearing of 90° or 270°. In practice, a good method for maintaining an arc is to fly a series of short legs, keeping the bearing pointer on or near the wing tip position while maintaining the desired range. With the bearing pointer on the wing tip and the aircraft at the desired range, maintain heading and allow the bearing pointer to move 5 to 10 degrees behind the wing tip position. This will cause the range to increase slightly. Next, turn toward the station to place the bearing pointer 5 to 10 degrees ahead of the wing tip, and maintain this heading until the bearing pointer is again behind the wing tip.

During crosswind conditions, the reference point (wing tip) will change. If the wind is blowing the aircraft away from the station, the reference point is ahead of the wing tip. If the wind is blowing the aircraft toward the station, the reference point is behind the wing tip.

Bank Angle Method:

$$r_{feet} = \frac{V_{TAS}^2}{11.26 \tan \phi}$$

$$r_{nm} = \frac{V_{TAS}^2}{(11.26)(6076) \tan \phi}$$

$$= \frac{V_{TAS}^2}{68416 \tan \phi}$$

$$\phi = \arctan \frac{V_{TAS}^2}{68416 \tan \phi}$$

The rule of thumb:

Bank angle to maintain an arc is the aircraft's turn radius times 30 divided by the arc distance.

Testing the rule of thumb against the formula above results in an error of only 1° of bank when flying less than 240 KTAS and is therefore validated.

14: SA

EC-135 Over Mt. Rushmore (USAF Photo)

As the wing's standardization crew, it was our responsibility to ensure every crewmember measured up to all regulatory standards and performed well enough to accomplish the mission. As the crew commander, it was my job to ensure Crew One performed to that standard. But who kept an eye on me?

Pacific Air Forces Headquarters had their own standardization office that was responsible for every standardization office in the command. Since the Pacific Air Forces was primarily a fighter command, each officer in the headquarters standards office was a fighter pilot. One of those pilots was tasked with giving me my check ride every year. They waited until I had exactly one year as the wing's chief of standardization to schedule the check and asked that I report to their offices on base.

I checked in at the front desk where the secretary assured me Captain Gibbs was free and I could walk right into his office. "Marke Gibbs?" I asked.

"Yes," she said. "I heard you two are acquainted." I peered into the office and there he was, looking just like I remembered him from pilot training, though a few pounds heavier.

"Eddie!" he said. "Imagine my surprise when we got your flight records and I saw your name."

"I had no idea you were in Hawaii," I said. "We should catch up."

"I just got here last week," he said. "The only reason they gave me your file is because I told them we know each other. Colonel Kyle is going to fly your check personally."

Marke explained that Colonel Kyle was the top flight examiner for the Pacific Air Forces and was losing patience with Lieutenant Colonel Spindler's frequent complaints. "Every time you bust somebody your squadron commander calls up with an appeal. He gets shot down every time but keeps calling. When your check ride came up he called to ask us to assign our meanest son bitch to take you down. We told him that would be Colonel Kyle."

"Is he?" I asked.

"Not at all," Marke said. "I think he has become a fan of yours. He said 'anyone who can deal with that crybaby for a squadron commander can't be too bad.' He's never been in the cockpit of a heavy before. I think he is considering the airlines and wants to see what a Boeing cockpit looks like."

Colonel Kyle met us at Base Operations and listened carefully as we briefed the flight, a four-hour sortie starting with air refueling south of Oahu with a tanker from the mainland. After that we would do instrument work at Kona on the Big Island before returning to Honolulu. He followed me as I inspected the exterior of the airplane, only speaking once. "She's a big sucker, isn't she?"

The departure was routine, meaning the sky was filled with airplanes. "I'm going to tighten the bank," I said right after takeoff, "to avoid that 747's wake. If you see something we don't see, Colonel, please point it out."

"Two light aircraft, ten o'clock," Jon said while pointing cross-cockpit. The colonel leaned forward from the jump seat.

"Cheezus," he said, "it's like a hornets nest." We finally left the insects behind as we flew to the air-refueling orbit area, about 100 miles south of Oahu. The standard orbit would have us fly inbound at 24,000 feet with the tanker heading in the opposite direction a thousand feet higher and about 12 miles further south. Ideally he would turn right in front of us, rolling out about 3 miles ahead.

"Tanker says they are at the control point," Carl said with his head buried in his radarscope, "but I don't see them." I turned in my seat to see Colonel

Kyle standing behind the navigator. "Wait a minute," Carl said. "They are at the wrong end of the orbit. Pilot turn left 30 degrees. Let's get them in the middle."

The tanker was nearly 50 miles south of course. Carl directed them to turn left 30 degrees to match our turn and got us joined up in the middle of the warning area. "I've never seen that done before," Kyle said, leaning between Jon and I. "Does this happen often?"

"The tankers aren't used to this kind of rendezvous," I said. "We see these mistakes now and then. Carl did a good job salvaging this. We could have wasted an hour chasing that tanker. This way it will cost us five or ten minutes, max."

We hooked up with the tanker, got our gas, and disconnected. "I need to verify disconnect capability before demonstrating the limits of the boom envelope," I said.

"Why do you have to demonstrate the limits at all?" Kyle asked. "Why not just keep it in the center. That's what we do in the F-15."

"Because moving an airplane this size in the envelope isn't intuitive," I said. "Control inputs are actually opposite what you would think because the airflow from the tanker affects the lift on our wings differently, depending on overlap."

"Show me," he said. He was full of questions and never failed to comment. "Well, I'll be. I would never have expected that."

After the refueling we headed to Kona where we had planned the majority of our pattern work. As Jon switched frequencies we heard approach control issue another airplane a clearance. "You are cleared for straight-in to Runway 17. Do you need any assistance, Lani Bird?"

"Ah, we might," the aircraft said. "Not sure the landing gear is fully extended. None of the lights are on and the airplane isn't flying straight."

"Lani bird?" I heard from the jump seat.

"Beech 99," Jon said. "They fly tour groups all over the island. They crash two or three a year. It sounds like the runway might get tied up. Maybe we should go someplace else."

"Good idea," I said. "See if you can get us to Maui."

"Center," Jon said on the frequency, "Mango zero one would like to get out of Kona's hair so they can better help Lani Bird. How about we go to Maui instead?"

"Everyone would appreciate that," Center said. "Turn left direct the Maui VOR. Thanks a lot guys!"

Jon and I alternated approaches and landings at the Kahului Airport on Maui until our requirements were met. As we made our last approach Colonel Kyle noticed the golf course just south of the airport. "Nice course," he said.

"Maui Lani," Jon said. "Back nine is better than the front."

I flew us back to Honolulu as the two golfers traded local course knowledge. I don't think either paid any attention for the remainder of the flight and the colonel didn't say anything to me at all until it was all over. We stood outside the airplane as the wing commander waited to drive Colonel Kyle off the flight line.

"Nicely done, Eddie," Colonel Kyle said. "You are going to be pleased with the written report." He turned to the wing commander. "These guys have SA worthy of fighter jocks and I only hope every airliner I fly has a crew with one-half their professionalism."

"Sierra hotel," the wing commander said, smiling.

The official check ride grade was "Exceptional," and breaking with protocol Colonel Kyle made a few extemporaneous comments about our situational awareness.

"Your SA might be exceptional in the airplane," Lieutenant Colonel Spindler said the next morning, "but it ain't worth a damn on the ground. You got a surprise coming, captain."

Boeing E-3 Sentry (USAF Photo)

I called the Military Personnel Center in Texas, asking if there had been any action on my record. "Sure has," the assignments officer said. "You have been approved for a transfer to Tinker Air Force Base in Oklahoma. You have a school date to transition to the E-3 AWACS."

"What if I don't want to do that," I asked.

"Your only option would be to separate," he said. "It's not such a bad job, captain. They are working hard to get the gone from home rate under 300."

Airborne Warning and Control System crews were based in Oklahoma but spent most of the year in the Middle East. Crews were burnt out from the flying and their families from the separation. They had the highest divorce rate in the Air Force. I contemplated divorcing the Air Force first, but the *Lovely Mrs. Haskel* counseled patience.

My next call was to Omaha and a captain I had only met once.

"How many hours do you have?" Captain Steve Kowalski asked. "We just had a guy bust his check ride with United and the next guy we had in line just separated from the Air Force. You might get lucky. Hold on, let me get Colonel Ellison."

"You want to fly a 747, Eddie?" Ellison asked.

"I do, sir," I said. "But I just got orders to AWACS."

"I can get those canceled," he said.

"I'm still short a couple of hundred hours," I said.

"I'll waive that," he said.

"When do I show up?" I asked.

"We have a class with United Airlines in two weeks," he said. "We can make this happen, but you have to promise to pass your check ride."

"I'll do that."

On Wednesday my orders to AWACS were cancelled.

On Thursday my orders to fly the Boeing 747 showed up. I was ordered to report into the 1st Airborne Command Control Squadron in one week and then to the United Airlines Training Center in Denver, Colorado the week after that. I was signed up for their Boeing 747 Captain upgrade class.

Situational Awareness (SA)

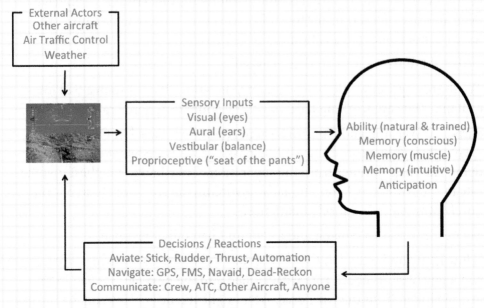

Sensory Inputs. A pilot's situational awareness requires an accurate perception of the environment and the aircraft. If you want to improve your SA, you need to ensure the channels of communications from your sensory inputs are unimpeded:

Visual. You visually acquire aircraft attitude, performance, navigation, and spatial information. You can improve all of these using technology, such as enhanced vision systems, heads up displays, radar, synthetic vision, and flight management systems.

Aural. You use your ears for the radio and the noise level of the cockpit can tell you volumes about airspeed, altitude, thrust settings, and aircraft health.

Vestibular. Your ears' semicircular canals derive attitude and rate of turn information, but this system is easily fooled.

Proprioceptive. The proprioceptive system reacts to the sensations resulting from pressures on joints, muscles, and skin and from slight changes in the position of internal organs. Forces act upon the seated pilot in flight. With training and experience, the pilot can easily distinguish the most distinct movements of the aircraft by the pressures of the aircraft seat against the body. The recognition of these movements has led to the term "seat-of-the-pants" flying. This system is also easily fooled.

Physiology. Not all of your inputs will be valid, it is up to the gray matter in your head to sort the wheat from the chaff:

Ability. You have ability, natural and trained, to process all those sensory inputs and to make that information useful.

Memory. There are three types of memory and all three can be trained. Your conscious memory controls most of your actions. Your muscle memory reacts to your will to perform basic tasks without taking too much consicous effort. Your subconscious memory is continually learning and producing the "feeling" you get which can be called intuition.

Anticipation. Your subconscious brain uses all sensory inputs and memory to anticipate the future. This anticipation is your situational awareness. You need to pay attention to the world around you and keep your mind alert to take advantage of the memory's internal database to maintain good SA.

Decisions / Reactions. Your conscious and subconcious team together to produce reactions based on your sensory inputs.

Aviate. You must always devote at least one pilot to flying the airplane and when SA begins to break down, it is usually wise to dedicate that pilot exclusively to the task of keeping the airspeed, altitude, and heading where they need to be. Automation can be a hinderance or a help, and where it is a hinderance the pilot must take over.

Navigate. The first priority in navigation is keeping the airplane from hitting anything and then comes getting the airplane to the destination if possible, any airport if necessary, and on the ground in one piece as a last resort. If the GPS is healthy that should be the "go to" source, followed by operative flight management systems, ground-based navigation aids, and back to basic dead reckoning.

Communicate. Keep the lines of communication in the cockpit open, the best ideas may be someone else's and discussion can produce solutions any single individual would have missed. Air traffic control, the home base, or the aircraft manufacturer are only a phone call away.

Action / Reaction Loop. Once the pilot has made a decision and acted, the result may be completely unexpected because the environment itself (weather, ATC, other aircraft, etc.) has a vote. The sensory inputs must again be assessed and the pilot must restart the action/reaction loop.

Clues of degraded situational awareness. If the airplane gets to some point in space and time before your brain does, you have lost situational awareness.

"What's it doing now?" — If the aircraft automation commands a change in aircraft horizontal or vertical navigation that surprises you, you either have an automation problem or you have lost SA.

"Why's it doing that?" — If an aircraft system starts to act up, it might be a systems-related problem. But it could also be a programming or other user input error due to the user's confusion caused by a loss of SA.

"I guess we are there" — If the airplane gets to an event sooner than you expected, for example if you get a vertical alert announcing the top of descent, you may have lost SA.

"It's awfully quiet on the radio" — If you are preoccupied in the cockpit and realize you haven't heard anything on the radio for a while, you or ATC may have missed a handoff. You have lost SA.

Situational Awareness Restoration Plan

Fly the airplane. Make sure one pilot is devoted to keeping the airplane right-side-up, the airspeed indicator above the stall and below the red line, the altimeter where it should be (usually that means level flight).

Make the automation make sense. Once you've evaluated the aircraft's attitude and speed trend, decide what part of automation is helping and what part is hurting. Take over the chores that aren't working.

Evaluate the big picture. It may be helpful to verbalize the situation from the very big picture to the smaller details as a way of getting your brain back into the game.

Buy time. If things are not going well, if you have enough fuel, and if there isn't a dire reason to get the airplane on the ground, look for a way to buy time. Ask for a holding pattern or delay vectors.

Communicate. It never hurts to ask for some help.

Step back and reassess. If your current view isn't helping, step back and take a look from another perspective. "What would Wilbur and Orville have done?"

Calm down. Take a breath and take stock of what you have going for you and what is working against you.

Hawaii Postscript

United Airlines Boeing 747 at 37,000 Feet (Steve Walsh, Creative Commons)

A week later I was sitting in cattle class of a United Airlines Boeing 747, headed east. A flight attendant tapped me on the shoulder. "Captain Haskel," she said. "You've been invited to the flight deck." I followed her forward and up the spiral staircase. Behind the cockpit door I found Second Officer Kevin Davies sitting at the flight engineer's panel. "I thought I saw you get on the airplane," he said. "I heard about your orders. You are going to love the seven four."

We traded stories of him loving life on the outside and me looking back on the 9th ACCS as the best five years of my life.

"Really?" he asked.

"Really," I said. "I started out as a copilot and ended up as an examiner. I learned more about flying in less time than I thought possible."

"You learned the meaning of it all, Eddie?"

"No," I said. "I learned that years ago. The meaning of it all is that your attitude toward learning determines your altitude as a person. That's old news. The new mystery is finding out the best way to learn. I somehow learned what I needed to know in Hawaii. But it wasn't easy and I'm not even sure how it happened."

"Well get ready to drink from a fire hose," he said. "United is going to shove more learning down your throat than you thought possible. I hated it." I said nothing and he thought.

"You're going to love it."

15: A New Ball Game

Stapleton, Denver CO

1986

United Airlines Boeing 747 (Aero Icarus – Creative Commons)

I checked into the Cherry Creek Hotel in Denver, Colorado because that's where all United Airlines crews stayed. The morning shuttle bus was filled with guys and gals who looked just like me, maybe a third had obvious military pedigrees. Everyone was carrying the large white envelope with the UAL logo that I knew included the "Welcome to the United Team!" letter. I scanned the thirty faces and found my target, the oldest guy on the bus.

"Pete?" I asked.

"Yes, sir," he said. "You must be Captain Haskel."

With that every head turned my way. I knew their first thoughts must have been 'captain?' How could a bus of new hires include a captain? Of course Master Sergeant Peter Kane was addressing me by my military rank.

"It's Eddie," I said. "We need to get through this together."

"You got that right," he said. "I heard the last crew got cremated here and their ashes got sent back to their old squadrons."

"That's not going to happen with us," I said.

We waited our turns with the rest of the group at the United Stapleton training center. But instead of being sent to the flight surgeon for step one of the process, we were handed three-ring binders each with a picture of a pretty United Boeing 747 in front with our names. Pete's said "Second Officer Kane" and mine said "Captain Haskel." As soon as it hit my hands it became

141

my favorite possession. We walked together to the third floor where Pete made a left turn and I turned right. I found the classroom and walked into a sea of geriatric pilots, ten or twelve wrinkled faces, each turned my way. Most quickly turned away and continued with whatever joke or war story that was already in progress.

"The first officer class is two doors down," the instructor said.

"This is my class," I said, raising my folder with the word "Captain" on the front.

"How old are you?" the instructor said. Now all conversation ceased.

"Thirty," I said. "I'm an Air Force pilot and Uncle Sam is paying United to teach me how to fly like a pro."

"Well come on in!" The hostility turned around on a dime, conversation resumed, and I was invited to sit up front. The instructor gave us flight manuals, a training guide, and a ten-page booklet with just three letters on the cover page: CRM.

"You guys know the drill," the instructor said. "Everyone here has been a captain on smaller equipment, we all know how to do this. Study the flight manual and training guide, you can look at the sound-on-slide shows in the library if you want, and come back one week from today for your written exams and simulator assignments."

"CRM?" someone from the back of the room asked.

"Oh yeah," he said. "Guys you gotta read the CRM manual. The test includes five CRM questions." There was a collective groan.

As the rest of the class made for the exit I did a quick inventory. The United flight manual looked like any Air Force flight manual, except it was printed with color pictures and appeared to be brand new. The training manual was completely foreign to me. It had instructions and drawings explaining how to do everything from takeoff to landing, removing all guesswork on how United wanted every single task completed. The CRM manual looked like something the lawyers put together. I had never heard of Crew Resource Management and the concept seemed to be completely unnecessary. How do you manage something that manages itself?

I looked up from my books and realized the classroom was empty. Even the instructor was gone. I collected my things and left, turning the lights off behind me. The library was equally deserted. I found the 747 corner and made myself comfortable. Each desk had a personal slide projector, cassette tape player, headset, and three shelves of lesson boxes. "Everything starts with the number one," I said to myself, pulling the box labeled "1 - Limitations."

Four hours later I felt a gentle nudge from behind. "You got the fuel system memorized yet?" It was Pete, holding his own stack of books. The slide show in front of me showed a schematic of the airplane's fuel vent system and the open box said "14 - Fuel."

"I guess not," I said. "I don't remember pulling this lesson from the shelf."

"That ain't good," he said. "We're spending the day talking electrics. They are teaching the test but I'm not learning the system the way I want. The Boeing is completely different than the Lockheed I grew up with. I need to understand how it works before I think about passing a test."

"Well at least they are teaching," I said. "My instructor is this projector here."

"Their instructors suck," Pete said.

After lunch Pete returned to class and I returned to my cubicle and contemplated the box with "9 – Electrical Power" on the spine. According to my notes I had already been through it once, but none of the knowledge took hold. Had I wasted the morning?

The United manual started off with pictures of switches, moved into diagrams of systems, and ended with descriptions of components. It was great reference material but did little to teach. "I am an instructor," I said to myself with my notebook turned to an empty page. Just as some non-airplane subjects lend themselves to topical, chronological, or other organizational methods, airplane systems are best understood thinking source-flow-user-output. The only sources of electricity in the 747 are the battery, the APU generators, and the engine generators. From there everything flows through switches, relays, buses, and fuses. The users are all the electrical components, each with their own form of output. Easy. In another four hours ten pages of notes were filled and I understood the Boeing 747 electrical system.

"All I really need is some time on the panel," Pete said that night at the bar. "I learn better with my hands than my brain. But if I don't pass the written I'll never see the sim. Damned Boeing."

"This is my third Boeing," I said, "and the engineer's panel makes more sense than any I've seen before. If you look at any system and think about water flowing in plumbing, it all makes sense."

"Water and electricity don't mix, college boy," he said.

"I know that," I said. "But if you think of everything flowing from top to bottom on that electrical panel, the connections between batteries, generators, and buses all work."

We spent the rest of the night talking electrons until the light bulb above Pete's head signaled he got it. Just as his light bulb illuminated mine went to a new level of intensity. I really understood. Over the next week we repeated the exercise until we knew that airplane from nose to tail. Pete scored a perfect 100. I missed three questions on CRM.

The next day we were treated to simulator session one with instructor David Santelli, a former Army helicopter mechanic turned pilot thanks to the Serviceman's Readjustment Act of 1944, the G.I. Bill. He was a thirty-year United veteran waiting out his time for retirement, happy to work only a few days a month in the simulator teaching. "You should have these flows down by now," he said after our first four-hour session.

"On day one?" I asked.

"This isn't the Air Force," he said. "This is a business, you either keep up or you get shown the door."

"I will do better," I said.

We repeated the "you should know this by now," "I will do better" cycle for the next week. I was always one step behind. Every session included a different guest copilot, usually another instructor from the training center, but not always 747 qualified. Qualified or not, every simulator session ended with a critique of my failure to lead the crew in an authoritative manner. After ten sessions we had covered everything at least once and Santelli announced Pete was ready for a check ride. He left my fate unmentioned.

The next day I was climbing nicely after the number three engine caught fire and was shut down. I was using all of the rudder trim to keep the airplane flying straight and was thinking about dumping fuel. As the altimeter crept through 3,000 feet the master caution light came to life with its annoying beep, beep, beep. I scanned the panel and saw the "Reverser Operating" light illuminated over the number four engine indicators. "Looks like we need the Inflight Reverse Thrust checklist, please," I said in the calm, "ah shucks" voice I had perfected with years of practice. "I don't think there's any additional yaw."

"Roger that," the guest copilot said, pulling the number four start lever to CUT OFF. The engine wound down and the left wing started to rise as I ran out of rudder.

"Relight it!" I yelled, running out of my allotment of calm. "Relight it now!"

Pete reached forward and moved the number four ignition switch to FLIGHT START. "Help Pete with the checklist," I said to the copilot. I nursed the pitch to keep our speed just above the stall and watched as the altimeter slowly unwound.

"Light off," Pete said. In my periphery I saw the red lights in the master caution panel extinguish one after another until we were left with the ones we started with, the number three engine shutdown. "You got it back."

I got the airplane on the ground and prepared for the bloodbath sure to come. As we sat in the debrief room I was prepared to take the blame for the copilot's mistake, but that never came. "Our old friend CRM again," Santelli said. "Eddie you have lousy command presence. 'May I have the checklist please?' What kind of an order is that? If you want a specific checklist, you bark that order out! Please? The only time you say please is if you want to empower the crew. If you have a reverser light, only you know if there is or isn't any yaw. With such a wishy washy captain, no wonder the copilot shut the engine down. If the captain isn't going to command, somebody has to."

I sat quietly, not knowing what to say. We had one simulator session left before the check ride, but that check ride would never come if I didn't get Santelli's vote of confidence. Arguing was out of the question.

"Eddie," he said to me as Pete listened quietly, "you have the typical Air Force pilot problem."

"How do I fix that?" I asked, letting the faulty premise slide.

"You Air Force pilots are used to having everything handed to you. You've never had to fight for a type rating. You get the glory but never have to pay your dues. And for all that you don't know how to run a crew. It is no wonder you missed all the CRM questions on your written."

His was a typical view among many pilots with military experience but without Air Force or Navy wings. By the time I was 22 I had almost 200 hours of jet experience, a pilot's license, and the exalted status of military aviator. If I passed the check rides to come, I would have an airline transport pilot's license with a Boeing 747 type rating. And it was all handed to me, Santelli would say, with zero effort on my part. I nodded quietly and left with Pete.

"You going to take that?" Pete asked, as we trudged to the crew bus through the season's first snow.

"I'll figure it out," I said. "I need him to sign me off for the check ride. Once I get that, I don't need him or his attitude."

That night I pulled out the United Airlines Crew Resource Management guide, something I should have done on day one. United studied their aircraft mishap history over the years and found an alarming number could have been prevented had the crew simply worked together as a team. The scenarios ran the gamut: the captain was overbearing and didn't listen to valid inputs from the crew, the captain couldn't make a decision and vacillated until it was too late, or the captain let the crew walk all over him and nothing got done. From the crew perspective things were just as bad. The crew knew there was a problem and never spoke up, fearing the captain's wrath. The crew was argumentative and failed to follow through on orders that could have saved the day. Or the crew withdrew completely and left the captain solo. I saw myself in every scenario. Maybe Santelli had a point.

A good captain, the United CRM report concluded, could slide easily from a dictator at one extreme all the way to being a good guy, team leader on the other. The key to success was knowing when the situation called for one style of leadership versus the other. When the airplane is threatened and things need to get done, the captain needs to be boss and rule with an iron hand. Sure he needs to listen, but there is no time for committee decisions. At other times, the captain is a mentor, an instructor, and a cheerleader. I had one more sim session to prove myself to Santelli.

The next day we were climbing out of San Francisco with a perfectly good airplane, passing 8,000 feet with no sign of trouble. It was a sure sign of trouble in a simulator. I scanned the instruments, again, and again. "How we doing, Pete?" I asked.

"No problems back here, captain." Just as he got the last syllable out there was the master caution chime with a single light.

"Forward cargo door light," Pete said.

"Let's level off at 10,000 feet," I said to the day's copilot. "Tell center we are returning to San Francisco."

"Pete," I said, "run the CARGO DOOR LIGHT ON checklist."

"You want me to go downstairs and take a look at the cargo door?" he asked. "Maybe it's just a light."

"No," I said. "Run the checklist." The procedure called for us to descend to 10,000 feet and equalize the cabin pressure with the atmosphere.

"Okay crew," I said once that was done. "My plan to is land overweight. The runway at San Francisco is dry and the data says we can do it. Does anybody have any better ideas or suggestions?"

"Works for me," Pete said.

"Me too," the copilot said.

Santelli flipped a few switches on his panel and there was a loud explosion. The number three engine fire light illuminated as its RPM indications wound down to zero. "Standing by the engine fire checklist," Pete said.

"Do it," I said, still wrestling with the controls. "Get us a vector to a three mile final," I said to the copilot.

"United One," the air traffic controller said, "expect a ten minute hold, we have higher priority traffic inbound."

"Tell them we are heading straight for the runway whether they like it or not," I said. "What they do with the other airplane is up to them."

We got the airplane on the ground and the session was over. I thanked the guest copilot before he left. "You did good," he said. "Don't let Santelli tell you otherwise. If you'd let the engineer go down to check the light, the cargo door would have blown then and he would have gone down the intake of the number three engine along with the door."

I hadn't thought of that but it seemed obvious after the fact. Santelli, for his part, wasn't so impressed. "Well you did better," he said. "But you still aren't up to United standards as far as I'm concerned. We'll see how you do on the oral before we commit to a simulator check. Just remember you are dealing with a Fed. The FAA isn't as forgiving and they notch up busts like trophies. Treat every question as if you are in court and answer only the question. If you keep from digging yourself into a hole you can get out in less than three hours."

I left the training center eager to return to the hotel, where I knew the *Lovely Mrs. Haskel* was waiting. She had stayed behind in Hawaii an extra three weeks to spend some time with both our families and to give me the extra time solo to study the new jet. I gave her the play-by-play of the day's simulator session and awaited her verdict.

"Treat every question as if you are in court?" she asked. "Is he serious?"

"I've heard that before," I said. "You don't want to volunteer anything that reveals a gap in your knowledge."

"Do you have any gaps?" she asked.

"I am sure I do," I said. "It's a big airplane."

"How would you react," she said, "if the shoe was on the other foot? If you were giving the check ride and the examinee played that legal game with you, wouldn't it piss you off?"

"Yeah," I said. "I guess it would."

"Be yourself, Eddie," she said. "It has always worked for you in the past."

That night I sat down with the 347 sample questions I had written for myself and started to read. The next morning the notebook was strewn on the hotel floor, open to question 238. Not bad.

The FAA flight examiner met me in the room set aside for the Feds. On the wall was a photo of the flight engineer's panel. It wasn't what I was expecting.

The examiner took my pilot's license, made a few notes on a form, and tucked the paperwork into his briefcase. I wouldn't see my license again

B-747-200SF Flight Engineer's Panel(Photographer: "Leftright," released to public domain)

until the process, all of it, was over to his satisfaction. If the oral went well, the next day we would fly a check ride profile in the simulator. If that went well, we would do it again in an actual airplane. I still didn't understand how my very first flight in an airplane could be a check ride but that was for the future. I still had an oral to pass.

"Tell me," he said pointing to the photo, "how this switch right here relates to the entire airplane. Don't skip any details." He was pointing to the battery switch, in the upper left side of the engineer's panel. I nodded and he sat down.

"That switch," I said, "is related to everything. We can look at every single system, from the top of its panel to the bottom, and find a cause and effect." And with that, the game was afoot. I spoke for about fifteen minutes about the electrical system and waited for a reaction. There was none. "The fuel system," I resumed, "can run without electrons but you need electricity for boosted pressure, to move fuel from tank to tank, and to direct the flow in any direction other than an engine's dedicated tank to its engine." The examiner nodded his head but said nothing. So I spoke for another hour, covering every single item on the panel. "And that," I said with a flourish, "is how the battery switch is related to the rest of the airplane."

"Excellent," he said. "Best oral I've ever heard. I guess I'll see you tomorrow in the box."

"But it's only been an hour and a quarter," I said. "I thought these were supposed to last three hours."

"You've covered everything," he said. "I can't imagine there being anything else. See you tomorrow."

I walked into Santelli's office. "You busted already?" he asked.

"No," I said. "Passed."

The simulator check was an anti-climatic cap to a month in the box, the examiner never saying a word until it was done. "See you in San Francisco," he said.

The next day, I was seated in the passenger lobby next to United's Gate One in San Francisco watching the Honolulu flight's passengers spill out of the jetway. "So that's what four hundred passengers on one jet looks like," Pete said.

"You get used to it," Santelli said. "Once they get her fueled, you hop in the left seat, I'll hop in the right, Pete at the panel. We'll take her to Sacramento and you get a four-engine approach to a missed, a three-engine approach to a missed, and a three-engine landing. That will conclude your training. We'll invite the Fed to the cockpit and you'll get a takeoff with an engine failure, a three-engine approach to a missed, and then a three-engine visual approach to a landing. If all that goes well, we come back to San Francisco for a four-engine landing. Maybe one of you Air Force guys is going to pass for a change."

Pete gave me a look and I grinned, willing him to keep his mouth shut.

Sitting in the cockpit, 28 feet above the tarmac and looking down on the passengers seated at Gate One, it finally hit me that I was about to fly the airplane of my dreams. I programmed the inertial navigation system as Santelli completed the interior inspection checklist from the right seat. Pete was outside with his instructor doing the exterior inspection.

"I'll be in back until you call," the FAA examiner said to Santelli.

The ground crew hooked up and asked for permission to push back. I

B-747-100 Cockpit (Oliver Cleynen – Creative Commons)

looked to Santelli. "Get us clearance with ground, please." He did so, turning an eyebrow down at the word "please."

Pete and Santelli got the engines started as I supervised from my regal perch, the master of the massive airplane. Taxiing the airplane was surprisingly easy, provided you trusted the taxiway lines made room for the 196 feet of wing. Departing runway 1 Right, the airplane leapt off the ground. As quick as I called for a checklist Pete would have it done. In less than 20 minutes we were on final to Runway 34 Right at Sacramento, one engine at idle to simulate an engine failure. The airplane flew better than the simulator. Two missed approaches later I was on final again, ready for my first landing.

Passing 50 feet I remembered Santelli's first words on simulator ride one: "at fifty get ready but don't do nothing." I didn't do nothing. "At thirty feet, gently pull back but don't stop the descent." The airplane complied with my slightest wishes. "At ten feet make sure you are still descending and get ready to give the runway a kiss." It was a kiss so tender, it would have made the *Lovely Mrs. Haskel* blush.

The biggest surprise was the stability of the airplane. There was absolutely no Dutch roll and even the strongest gusts of wind were handled by the airplane itself. "How dare you upset this wing," the big Boeing seemed to say. "This is a Boeing 747; such shenanigans are beneath us." Us, the royal pronoun. The airplane and pilot had this wired.

With that the examiner came forward and the fight was on. Santelli played his role as the competent first officer and each maneuver was better than the one before. Two hours after we started we rolled back into Gate One at San Francisco. I looked down to the terminal below, where a collection of passengers were waiting for the airplane's next journey back to Hawaii.

"You going to sit there all day?" Santelli asked. "Some of us got things to do."

I unstrapped and met the examiner downstairs in the forward galley. His paperwork was laid out on the counter. He had only one question. "How old are you, son?"

"Thirty."

"Well congratulations," he said. "You are the youngest person I've ever given a 747 type to." He shook my hand and gestured for me to sign my airline transport pilot's license with the world's best type rating.

Crew Resource Management

CRM History

[Kanki, Ch 1.] In the early years, the image of a pilot was of a single, stalwart individual, white scarf trailing, braving the elements in an open cockpit. This stereotype embraces a number of personality traits such as independence, machismo, bravery, and calmness under stress that are more associated with individual activity than with team effort.

When airplanes required two, three, and even four pilots, problems arose from pilots not working together or simply not taking advantage of crew synergies.

[Kanki, §1.4.4] A 1979 NASA study placed 18 airline crews in a Boeing 747 simulator to experience multiple emergencies. The study showed a remarkable amount of variability in the effectiveness with which crews handled the situations. Some crews managed the problems very well, while others committed a large number of operationally serious errors. The primary conclusion drawn from the study was that most problems and errors were introduced by breakdowns in crew coordination rather than by deficits in technical knowledge or skills.

CRM Decision Making Continuum

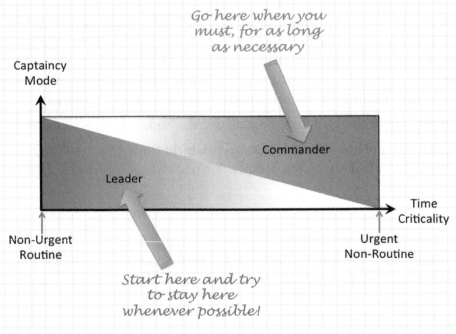

Consider the Captain

[CRM Handbook, pg. 25.] Effective leaders perform four primary functions:

1) Regulating Information Flow. The leader must regulate, manage, and direct the flow of information, ideas, and suggestions within the cockpit crew and between the cockpit crew and outside sources. This includes: Communicating flight information, asking for opinions, giving opinions, clarifying communication, providing feedback, regulating participation.

2) Directing and Coordinating Crew Activities. The leader must function as crew manager to provide orientation, coordination and direction for group performance. This includes: directing and coordinating crew activities, monitoring and assessing crew performance, providing planning and orientations, setting priorities, delegating tasks.

3) Motivating crewmembers. The leader must maintain a positive climate to encourage good crewmember relations and to invite full participation in crew activities. This includes: creating proper climate, maintaining an "open" cockpit atmosphere, resolving/preventing conflict, maintaining positive relations, providing non-punitive critique and feedback.

4) Decision-making. The leader is ultimately responsible for decisions. This includes: assuming responsibility for decision making, gathering and evaluating information, formulating decisions, and implementing decisions.

Decision Making

[CRM Handbook, pg. 23.] The decision making process:

1) Recognizing or identifying the problem. Does a problem exist that requires action?

2) Gathering information to assess the situation. Determining what information is needed, who has the needed information, and whether the information is verified by other crewmembers and resources.

3) Identifying and evaluating alternative solutions. Evaluating the advantages as well as the risks associated with each alternative identified, and selecting the optimum alternative.

4) Implementing the decision. Executing the decision and providing feedback on actions taken to crewmembers.

5) Reviewing consequences of the decision. Evaluating the consequences of the decision and revising the decision if consequences are not as anticipated.

Consider the Crew

[Cortés] Regardless of what tone has been set by the captain, crewmembers have an obligation to be assertive and to voice concerns and opinions on matters of importance to the safety of the flight.

But what happens when a crewmember needs to convey important information and the captain is not listening, or does not grasp the importance or critical nature of what the crewmember is attempting to convey? To deal with such situations, the industry has adopted a 5-step assertiveness process.

1. Get the captain's attention (use name or crew position): "Jim, I have a concern I want to discuss with you."

2. State the concern: "I am not comfortable with this heading that we are on."

3. State the problem and consequences: "If we continue on this heading, we will be too close to the buildup."

4. Give solutions:"I think we should turn 20 degrees further west."

5. Solicit feedback and seek agreement: "What do you think?" or "Don't you think so?"

[CRM Handbook, pg. 20.]

Accident reports reveal a number of instances in which crewmembers failed to speak up even when they had critical flight information that might have averted a disaster. In most cases, this hesitancy involved a copilot or flight engineer who failed to question a captain's actions or to express an opinion forcefully to the captain. These types of incidents lead to the conclusion that crewmembers are often unwilling to state an opinion or to take a course of action, even when the operation of the airplane is clearly outside acceptable parameters.

Assertive behavior includes:

- Inquiry: inquiring about actions taken by others and asking for clarification when required.

- Advocacy: the willingness to state what is believed to be a correct position and to advocate a course of action consistently and forcefully.

- Assertion: stating and maintaining a course of action until convinced otherwise by further information.

16: Aim Point

Offutt Air Force Base, Omaha, Nebraska

1986

E-4B Nightwatch (USAF Photo)

The 1st Airborne Command Control Squadron was the biggest secret on base. It had one of the largest buildings, one of the largest barbed wire fences, one of the largest contingents of armed security, and certainly the largest airplanes. You couldn't fail to see the three Boeing 747s, what the Air Force called E-4Bs, towering over the flight line, as well as the fourth shooting touch and go landings in the distance. It was déjà vu all over again from my first day at the 9th ACCS, so many years ago. The guard judged my paperwork with suspicion and never let up until my sponsor appeared opposite the fence.

"Major," I said while saluting the lanky officer in the neatly ironed blue shirt.

"It's Frank," he said, returning the salute. "I heard you passed your check ride. You got an honest to goodness ATP I take it?"

"Yeah," I said. "They'll give them to anyone these days. They hand them out like candy."

"I didn't get one," Frank said. "Neither did the guy before me. You're gonna get a different reception than we did." Major Frank Court explained that the squadron commander believed the Airline Transport Pilot's license divided the men from the boys and he would have sent the boys home to the lesser squadrons that produced them if he could. I looked for signs I might have offended him with my careless joke. I thought I was being self-deprecating when in fact I might have been sticking a poker in an open wound. "This is a great squadron," he said, "even for us second class citizens."

The squadron was unlike any I had ever been a part of or even seen from afar. The building was spotless, the walls were clean, and everything on those walls was professionally framed. Every person I saw was dressed right out of the regulations, had hair neatly combed within Air Force standards, and each wore a smile right out of a recruiting poster.

"I'll drop you off at the commander's office," Frank said, "but don't leave there without an escort. You can't go anywhere in this building without a Patriot Blue."

"Patriot who?" I asked.

"Never mind," he said.

I walked into Lieutenant Colonel Don Ellison's office, my right arm cocked and ready for the sharpest salute he had ever seen, but he intercepted me by grabbing my saluting hand.

"Shit hot, Eddie," he said, pumping my hand hard enough to make it ache. "You got a Boeing 747 type at the age of 30. Funny how in a squadron of majors and lieutenant colonels only two captains seem to have figured it out lately. You and Steve are going to get along fine."

"When do we get started, sir?" I asked.

"That's up to Alton," he said. "Nobody turns a wheel around here without Alton. Now tell me about your check ride. Don't leave out any details."

We sat in his office for an hour, two pilots trading war stories and talking about the Boeing 747. Ellison, I knew, had a resume as long as my arm that included the B-52 bomber, the RC-135 spy airplane, and more time in the Boeing 747 than any other pilot in the Air Force. I had a total of 2.5 hours in the jet. His black, thinning hair was combed straight back from a mafia movie and every hand gesture stirred thoughts of Al Pacino in a flight suit. I started to think of Colonel Ellison as my personal godfather.

After an hour the colonel released me and Frank escorted me through the squadron ready room up to another office with a large glass window. Inside I could see the standard scheduling board, but it was unlike any I had ever seen before. There were no crews, only crew positions. From top to bottom there were rows for instructor pilots, aircraft commanders, copilots, flight engineers, and flight attendants. At the bottom of the copilot section I found my name, just after Frank's. There were no flights scheduled for either of us. "The communicators, guards, and crew chiefs are handled by another office," Frank explained. "You wait here and I'll make sure Alton doesn't have any TSS you can't see."

"TSS?" I asked.

"Top secret shit," he said. Frank entered the office and said something to Lieutenant Colonel Alton Gee, the oldest lieutenant colonel I had ever seen. His hair was the grayest shade of gray and he had more mileage on his wrinkled face than I had seen on anyone not addressed as "grandpa." Colonel Gee closed a three-ring binder with the unmistakable image of the White House and the words "Patriot Blue" on top. He gestured me to enter.

"Captain," he said, still seated. "Your file says you are a real live engineer from Purdue. Is that right?"

"Yes, sir," I said.

"Well I got one question and one question only for you. Are you ready, son?"

"Yes, sir." He pulled out a clean sheet of lined paper and drew the unmistakable outline of a tree. "The town says I got to trim the tallest tree on my property because it violates some damned ordinance that says nobody's tree can be taller than 200 feet. Can you believe that? But I'm not about to climb that tree, even though I know it ain't no 200 feet high. So I measured 100 feet away from the tree and I took my protractor from the seventh grade and sighted up to the top and came up with an angle of 60 degrees. So how tall is my tree?"

Colonel Gee held a scientific calculator, ready to calculate. I looked at his face for signs this was a joke and, coming up empty, looked at the drawing. "You know two legs of a triangle but not the hypotenuse," I said. "The tangent of your angle is equal to the opposite leg divided by the adjacent leg. So your tree's height is equal to 100 times the tangent of 60 degrees."

Gee punched at his calculator and smiled. "We now know with the power of the great Purdue University that my tree is 173 feet high. Very good." He leaned back in his chair, waved to the scheduling board that appeared to be his personal kingdom, and then cast his gaze on me. "Now, what can I do for you?"

"Colonel," I said, "I am here to fly."

"My friends call me Alton," he said. "My enemies call me colonel. Which one will it be?"

"Alton," I said, "I am here to fly."

"Fly," he said, "you shall." With the stroke of his grease pencil, I had two training flights scheduled each week for a month.

"Now all I need is a flight manual and a training syllabus," I said to Frank as he escorted me from Alton's office.

"Our manuals officer is the newest nav," Frank said. "I saw him in the navigator's office." I followed Frank two doors down the hallway and was greeted by a face from my past.

"I knew it was only a matter of time before we got you in this squadron," Captain Mark Honable said, rising from his desk. "Good to see you after all these years."

"Ditto," I said. "Maybe we can avoid getting captured this time." Mark laughed and rose to shake my hand and then turned to a tall cabinet against the wall. Frank looked at us, waiting for an explanation. "Mark and I were paired together at survival school," I said. "He knows his way around a mountain."

Mark handed over a stack of technical orders, a book of regulations, and a form with my name already filled out. I recognized most of the regulations and the technical orders appeared to be volumes of the thickest flight manual I had ever seen. "What about a training guide?"

Frank and Mark laughed. "Eddie," Mark said, "this squadron doesn't do training guides or lesson plans. Welcome to the majors."

"Guys just kind of show up for the flight and the instructors instruct," Frank explained.

"How do I know how to prepare?" I asked.

"You don't," he said.

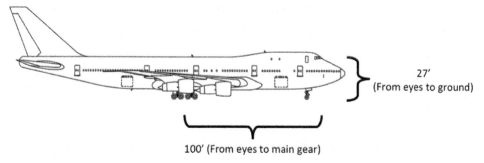

B-747 In a 3-point attitude (B-747 from Julien Scavini, Creative Commons)

Climbing the three flights of stairs from ground level to the cockpit it finally hit me just how high off the ground my new office would be. Sitting in the pilot's seat I craned my head against the windshield for a peak at the wing tips.

"You won't see nothing back there," Major Tom Polanshek said from the right seat. "You get used to it."

"How do you know your wings are clear of obstacles when you taxi?" I asked.

"Faith," he said.

Tom was pretty easy going, for an ex-baby killer. He grew up flying B-52 bombers and then graduated to the supersonic FB-111. He did well enough in bombers to name his next assignment and picked the E-4B.

"Remember the body gear is going to turn left when you move the tiller to the right," he said as I nudged the four throttles forward to begin our trek from in front of the squadron to the runway. "The airplane pivots on an axis about the main gear so the tail is whipping as quickly as the cockpit, only in the opposite direction."

From engine start, taxi, takeoff, all the way to 50 feet behind the tanker, Tom provided an answer to every question I had, before I could ask. "Don't move the throttles," he said after I called stabilized behind the tanker. "Just put a little pressure and wait. We weigh about three times as much as the airplane you used to fly, so we got three times as much inertia. It's what the engineers call a linear relationship."

"F equals m times a," I said.

"Something like that," he said.

Tom's instructional technique was excellent and the learning came easy until the first landing. I had us set up for my first landing at Andrews Air Force Base, Maryland. "Shift your aim closer to brick one," he said.

"Really?" I said.

"Yeah," he said, "we aim for the first set of markers, 500 feet down the runway."

"Where's that put our wheels?" I asked.

"The airplane is only 225 feet long, Eddie," he said. "Don't worry about it."

I pushed the nose down and pulled some power, waiting for the fixed point on the windshield to creep back. When things looked right — that is when things looked like we were aimed well short — Tom was happy. "Perfect," he said.

"I see a pattern of sixteen wheel prints in the overrun," I said. "Only one airplane in the world has that pattern."

"Ask Steve Kowalski about that," he said. "Just remember to flare and you'll be fine."

There are few things in aviation more fun than landing a Boeing 747. Even when aiming well short of what I was taught at United, it still generated an unstoppable grin. "Very nice," Tom said after our five-hour training sortie. "I think a couple more of these and you will be ready for a check." My training record was 100 percent praise followed by what might as well have been 100 percent criticism. "Needs to work on proper aim point."

$$h = 27 + \tan(5°) \times 100' = 36'$$

B-747 In a landing attitude (B-747 from Julien Scavini, Creative Commons)

Training sortie number two was just like number one, except at night. The instructor was just as good with the same advice on landing. "Aim for 500 feet," Major Mark Thomas said," that's what everyone does now."

"Now?" I asked.

"Yeah," he said. "We used to aim for brick one but Steve proved we couldn't do that. So now we aim for 500 feet. That way if we do something stupid, like forget to flare, at least our wheels will touch down on pavement."

"I don't think I understand the math," I said. "If you are aiming 500 feet forward and your wheels are 100 feet behind you, I think you still come up short. The flight manual says aim for 1,500 feet."

"The flight manual is wrong," he said. "When you get your Patriot Blue you'll find out we need to put this airplane onto some short runways."

"Okay," I said. "I'll try it your way, but it sounds like a good way to break something. I'd feel better about this if I had something in writing."

"We'll talk about this after the flight. And forget I mentioned Patriot Blue."

"Patriot who?" I asked.

"Exactly," he said. The photocopied form that followed me from flight to flight was slowly but surely filling with check marks. I stole a look at the single sheet of what appeared to be hand drawn lines and typed entries. I still had three or four items left, including the all important landing.

After the last bit of paperwork was done Mark pulled out a blank sheet of paper and I got ready for my aim point education. He started to draw a stick figure 747 but then stopped as Major Tom Polanshek entered the room. "Guess what I heard?" he said to Mark. "The promotion list is on base."

"Any advance intel?" Mark asked.

"I heard we all made it," Tom said. "You, me, and Greg. Our squadron cleaned house."

"Three new lieutenant colonels!" Mark said. "It had to be. When you are flying a White House mission on a Boeing 747, you got to get promoted!"

They both left, beaming. I sat alone with the drawing of the stick figure 747, wondering what to do. Captain Steve Kowalski appeared from the scheduler's office. "Aim point issues?" he asked.

"Yeah," I said. "I don't see how aiming this airplane at 500 feet is going to keep us on the runway. But I guess your experience has to prove something."

"It doesn't prove squat," he said. "I was aiming for 500 feet when I got the overrun at Andrews. I was trying to show the airplane was okay with a minimal flare, and it was." He paused for my reaction. "Except for not being on the runway, of course." Steve ended every sentence with a wry look, as if delivering the punch line to a packed house at an improv session. I was an audience of one.

"So why is that?" I asked. "If your eyes are aimed for 500 feet and the wheels are only 100 feet behind you, why did they end up short? Those wheel prints were halfway into the overrun, which puts them 1,000 feet short of your aim point."

"I don't know," he said. "You tell me."

Sortie three became four and five, and threatened to become six and seven. On sortie five I threw in the towel and adopted the 500-foot aim point and was recommended for a check ride with the squadron's evaluator pilot, Major Greg White. Greg kept his mouth shut throughout the check ride and after my fourth landing announced I had passed with flying colors.

"Really?" I asked. "No debrief, no long wait pacing the hallways, no having to guess the evaluator's body language?"

"Nah," he said. "We are all grown ups here. Besides, I need to steal a few landings. I have an interview with United coming up."

Greg revealed that he was going to turn down his promotion to lieutenant colonel and jump to the airlines. "Mark and Tom have lost sight of the goal," he said. "We are all aiming to be professional pilots after our time in the Air Force. Lieutenant colonels don't get to fly and they are hoping to make a twenty-year Air Force career in the cockpit. That doesn't happen these days. They forgot what they were aiming for."

He took the next three landings in the pattern, each landing aimed at the 1,000-foot fixed-distance marker. Each of his landings was right where he aimed, even after his textbook perfect landing flares.

"You aimed for 1,000 feet and that's where the wheels ended up," I said. "Everyone else tells me to aim for 500."

"I can't explain it," he said. "But in this airplane your wheels end up at your aim point after a flare. It didn't happen that way in smaller airplanes but it does on this one. I always thought aiming for brick one was silly and maybe dangerous. But that's what the squadron preached until Kowalski's screw up. Now they all aim for 500 feet."

"Except you," I said.

"Yeah," he said. "But when you get to be the senior evaluator you get to fly by your own rules."

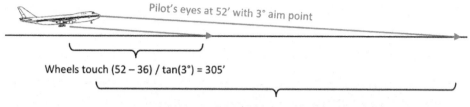

B-747 landing geometry (B-747 from Julien Scavini, Creative Commons)

That night I studied the aircraft flight manual for clues but only came up with the fact the pilot's eyes would be 52' above the runway when the aim point was within 1,000 feet on a 3-degree glide path. Since I knew the wheels were 36 feet below the pilot in a normal approach deck angle, the rest should be straightforward trigonometry. The math was straightforward but the conclusion was not. How could the wheels be aimed nearly 800 feet short of the pilot's eyes when the wheels were only 100 feet further back?

Basic flight instructors have always preached to their students about the importance of keeping the aim point stationary on the cockpit windscreen. "If that spot doesn't move," they would say, "that's exactly where your wheels are going to touch!" But was that true?

No, I suddenly realized. It was a lie. If your eyeballs were flying through space, then it would be true. But as pilots the wheels are not only behind you, they are underneath you too. We should not have been aiming for brick one, 500 feet, or even a thousand feet. In a Boeing 747, the aim point should have been just as United had taught us, at 1,500 feet. Our aim points were short of where they should have been.

The next morning the lieutenant colonel promotion list was released. Every major without staff experience was passed over. Our three hopefuls would have one more try and then be tossed out of the Air Force with nothing. They had aimed too far and had fallen short.

Aim Versus Touch Down Points

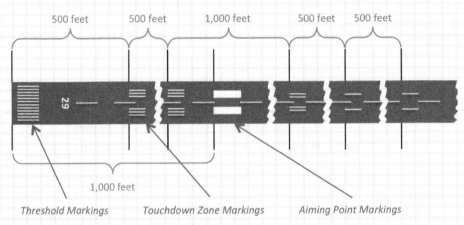

Threshold Markings   Touchdown Zone Markings   Aiming Point Markings

Runway Touchdown Zone Markings

[Aeronautical Information Manual, ¶2-3-3.e.] The touchdown zone markings identify the touchdown zone for landing operations and are coded to provide distance information in 500 feet (150m) increments. These markings consist of groups of one, two, and three rectangular bars symmetrically arranged in pairs about the runway centerline, as shown in [the figure]. For runways having touchdown zone markings on both ends, those pairs of markings which extend to within 900 feet (270m) of the midpoint between the thresholds are eliminated.

Runway Aim Point Markings

[Aeronautical Information Manual, ¶2-3-3.d.] The aiming point marking serves as a visual aiming point for a landing aircraft. These two rectangular markings consist of a broad white stripe located on each side of the runway centerline and approximately 1,000 feet from the landing threshold, as shown in [the figure].

[ICAO Annex 14, Volume I, §5.2.5] An aiming point marking shall be provided at each approach end of a paved instrument runway where the code number is 2, 3 or 4. (Runways 800m or longer.)

The aiming point marking shall commence no closer to the threshold than the distance indicated, except that, on a runway equipped with a visual approach slope indicator system, the beginning of the marking shall be coincident with the visual approach slope origin.

An aiming point marking shall consist of two conspicuous stripes.

Eye Wheel Height

The airplane's touch down point depends on where the wheels are in rela-
tion to your eyes, the things doing the aiming. The answer varies with
different aircraft. We'll use the Gulfstream 450 as an example.

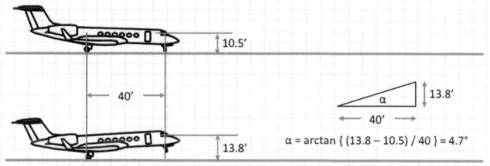

Using data found in aircraft manuals we find the distance between the landing gear and the pilot (40') and the distance between the pilot's eyes and the
pavement in a 3-point attitude (10.5'). A Gulfstream study reveals the pilot's
eyes will be 13.8' off the pavement when in the touchdown attitude. If your
manual does not provide this information, you can estimate it using the
aircraft's approach deck angle.

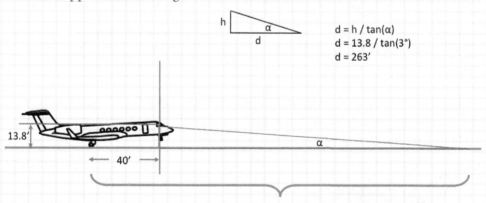

Main Gear to Aim Point = 263 + 40 = 303'

We can use basic trigonometry to determine the distance from our eyes
to an aim point. In the case of a three degree glide path, our G450 pilot's
eyes will be 263' behind the aim point, which means the wheels will be 303'
behind the aim point. As a general rule of thumb, your aim point will be
ahead of your wheels by seven times the distance between your wheels and
your eyes.

Flare Distance

The round out from approach deck angle to landing flare is heavily dependent on pilot technique. If you frequent runways short enough to require close examination of your landing distance charts, you ought to have a good idea how much runway your flare technique consumes. The Gulfstream 450 performance numbers, for example, are based on a very firm landing with the airplane coming down at 6 feet per second (360 fpm) with a flare that begins at 20 feet. If you simply allowed the airplane to hit the runway at that rate, the distance from the 20 foot height would be easy to compute:

$$\text{Distance from 20' without a flare} = \frac{20 \text{ feet}}{\tan(3°)} = 382 \text{ feet}$$

If we instead cut the rate of descent from 600 fpm to 100 fpm and allow the airplane to hit at that rate, the entire 20 feet averages out to $(600 + 100) / 2 = 350$ fpm:

$$\text{Time to descend 20' at average sink rate} = 20 \text{ feet} \; \frac{60 \text{ sec}}{350 \text{ feet}} = 3.43 \text{ sec}$$

The distance covered in 3.43 seconds at 125 KCAS:

$$\text{Distance in the flare} = 3.43 \text{ secs} \; \frac{125 \text{ nm}}{1 \text{ hr}} \; \frac{6076 \text{ ft}}{1 \text{ nm}} \; \frac{1 \text{ hr}}{3600 \text{ sec}} = 723 \text{ ft}$$

Using this technique, flaring to 100 fpm, we see that a G450 can be landed before its aim point and we can infer any larger flare will cause the airplane to land beyond its aim point.

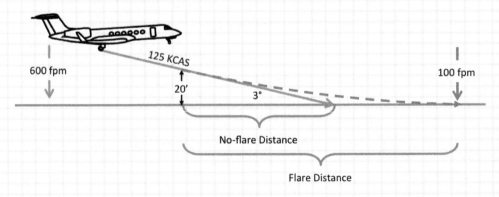

166

17: A Different Approach

E-4B Over Washington, D.C. (USAF Photo)

The day after the lieutenant colonel promotion board results were released, the Air Force announced it had a dire pilot shortage and that all of us captains would be getting $12,000 bonuses each year for agreeing to stay in until our 14 year points. Majors and lieutenant colonels would be getting nothing. As a copilot I was getting paid more than most of the aircraft commanders, instructor pilots, and every navigator except Alton Gee. The passed over majors started slinking around the squadron as if they had targets painted on their backs.

"Maybe they'll let us stay in as majors until we get twenty," Mark Thomas said. "That way we can retire, stay current, and collect a pension with the airlines."

"I'm not worried about it," Tom Polanshek said. "They are so desperate for pilots they are throwing money at the captains. We'll get promoted on the second try."

"You're dreaming," Greg White said. "They are going to screw us the first chance they get."

As the debate raged, I was called over to the Office of Special Investigations

167

to receive my upgraded security clearance. The office was hidden away in a part of the base I had never seen before, literally locked away in a vault. After signing three documents and giving ten fingerprints, I was escorted into the vault.

"Welcome to Patriot Blue," the major without wings said. "As this is your first code word clearance I must make the point that even the term Patriot Blue is classified and if you ever hear it outside of a secure area or from someone without the clearance, you must report it immediately. Got that?"

"Yes, sir." I said. He handed me four binders, one for each code word clearance I was about to receive. In the next hour I learned that our squadron had a code word mission with three cover stories. The cover story for the press was that we were flying a backup airplane for the President of the United States, which explained why one of our airplanes was always very near the man himself and why we spent so much time in Washington, D.C. There was another cover story for our families and a third for the United States Air Force.

"Not even the Air Force knows what we are really doing?" I asked the mysterious major.

"Nope. And it's your job to keep it that way, captain. Remember that not even the wing commander knows about your squadron's relationship with the White House. As far as he knows, your mission is what the second cover story says it is."

The only change to my official life was that I no longer needed an escort to walk around the squadron or within the airplane. For the first time I was allowed to view the aircraft cabin aft and below the cockpit. But that hardly mattered, I had no flying scheduled for a month.

"What's a newly qualified pilot got to do to fly around here?" I asked the one man in the squadron who could answer.

"Funny you should ask," Alton said. "Follow me."

Alton got up and led me out of his office into the next room, the door of which was marked "Nav Planning." The room had a single desk atop which stood a North Star Horizon computer, a huge machine with a green-on-black screen capable of 80 lines of text, and two 5-1/4 inch floppy disk drives. Alton sat at the desk, flipped on the power switch and the screen blinked on with a single message: "Wait."

Alton talked as he brought the squadron's navigation program to life, which appeared to be written in BASIC, a programming language I had only seen on my handheld calculator. The program asked single-line questions and Alton typed in the answers. "We are flying a mission to London next week," he said while fumbling with an en route chart, "might as well get something done while showing you the ropes." After about thirty minutes of this, the screen blanked again and said, "Go get a cup of coffee; this is going to take a while . . ."

"You drink coffee, *Ed-you-el?*" I nodded and Alton led me to the coffee bar. I knew that being awarded a pet name from Alton elevated me to a new level of esteem in the squadron. But it still left me in a fog as to why I was getting the navigator indoctrination.

"Old Frederick Fitz was a navigator of yore who was as useless as tits on a bull, but he knew computers," Alton said over his paper cup of Folgers. "Fit-zee wrote that program and convinced the squadron commander to get us the computer. It used to take us two hours to do a flight plan, now we can do one in about an hour. Pretty good, don't you think? Old Fitz is gone but his legacy lives on in that machine."

About half an hour later there was a flight plan hanging down from the dot matrix printer on five pages of perforated paper. Alton ripped the sheet with gusto and announced, "Here it is, our flight plan done at the speed of light." He scanned the output happily until about halfway down the second page, "Dammit, I missed a point." He checked the output versus the en route chart. "Now I got to start over."

I was looking for a graceful exit point. Looking at this computer was worth about five minutes of my interest, getting an understanding of how the navigators did their flight planning was worth the hour, but now we were moving into the waste of effort category. "Not that you need to stick around for all that," Alton said, as if reading my mind. "But you get the idea of why we need you to fix this."

"What?" Alton looked at me with puzzlement at first, sympathy second, and finally amusement. "Didn't you know we hired you because we heard you know all about this bits and bytes stuff?"

"No, but . . ."

"We got a copy of the program you wrote in Hawaii," Alton said. "We want one of those for our airplane." I stood there, motionless.

"Come on, *Ed-you-el*," Alton said while putting an arm around me and leading me out of the office, "you don't think we hired you because you are a good pilot? Hell, this man's Air Force is filled with good pilots. Now, find me a good programmer who can fly, well now you got something."

I spent a day or two sulking but that passed. Bruised ego aside, it seemed that if programming skills got me into the squadron, so be it. I had been looking for an excuse to learn the Pascal programming language and it would seem I had ample time. The Pascal language had nothing to do with mathematician Blaise Pascal, other than an admiration for efficiency and strict procedures. I bought the Turbo Pascal compiler for thirty dollars and went to work.

The program I wrote in Hawaii had an interface just as clunky as the Fitz version: it asked the user a series of questions before doing the actual work. One advantage my program had over Old Fitz's was mine saved the information so the navigator didn't have to start over after every attempt. It also ran faster only because the code was written with subroutines; it was compact by comparison. I didn't know BASIC well enough to fix the Fitz program, so I started over with Pascal and emulated a spreadsheet model, something like the wildly successful Lotus 123. It was fun. Because my program was compiled — compacted from Pascal instructions to machine code — it was lightning fast. No more "get a cup of coffee" messages.

Two months later the navigators were producing flight plans in ten minutes instead of an hour and the squadron was finally flying me on a regular basis. I started to think of myself as a pilot again; albeit a more humble pilot.

The day after the squadron's navigators accepted my navigation program, I was trying to circle our very large airplane into a very small runway in Waterloo, Iowa. The weather was at minimums and I was counting down the distance to the runway. At 2.3 nautical miles I would be allowed to start the maneuver. "I got nothing," I said to Steve Kowalski.

"Me neither," he said. "No, there it is."

I saw the faint lights of what was probably the runway. The runway's medium intensity approach lights cut through the fog, but just barely. I dipped a wing to offset us from the runway, looking for a downwind leg wide enough to make the turn to final possible, but still keep within the 2.3 nautical mile limit. Our minimum descent altitude was 1,480 ft. just 600 ft. above the terrain.

"We are really tight," I said. "I'm not sure this is going to work."

"You're doing fine," Steve said. The runway was on our right and I was relying on Steve's eagle eyes to keep sight of the airport environment. "Have faith."

"I don't like relying on faith," I said. "Besides, faith isn't much help with an overshooting crosswind." The stopwatch on my panel told me it was time to turn but I knew it would be futile. Our turn radius, combined with the wind, meant we would overshoot for sure.

"Start your turn," Steve said. "This is going to work just fine." I rolled into 30° of right bank, 5° more than the book recommended but right at the limits for flying in instrument conditions. "More bank," he said.

"I'm at thirty," I said.

"I'm visual with the runway," he said, "more bank!" The 747 is very stable and with a flick of my wrists the bank increased to 40° and stayed there. I pulled back slightly to add G-force into the turn. At long last I saw the runway. "Perfect," he said.

I wasn't so sure about perfection, but I landed the airplane. Steve signed off my last requirement before flying a presidential support mission and the next week we were both in March Air Force Base, near Riverside, California. President Reagan was at his California home, Rancho del Cielo, and we would be up the mountain doing a combination of one of our cover stories and the real Patriot Blue mission. "Explain to me again why we are here?" I asked.

"We fly where Whamo tells us," Steve Kowalski said. "That's all we really need to know."

The White House Military Office, "Whamo," called our shots and for this week it meant spending a week in California at March Air Force base, home to a wing of B-52 bombers and KC-135 tankers. The runway was over 13,000 feet long; I couldn't help comparing it to the postage stamp we used for circling in Iowa.

"Why does it take 40° of bank to circle this thing?" I asked during a morning preflight, "when the book says 25° should work and all the other numbers were within limits?"

"You tell me," Steve said. It was his standard answer to everything. I spent the day with the books, looking for an answer. Our 747 was in circling approach category D, which meant if we kept our speed below 166 knots and stayed within 2.3 nautical miles of the runway, we wouldn't hit anything. The same FAA regulation required 2 miles of visibility to legally fly most of these circling approaches, including the one at Waterloo that was consuming an unhealthy part of my thoughts during REM sleep.

The rules said we must always keep sight of the runway when circling. Our civilian and military approaches are designed according to the United States Standard for Terminal Instrument Procedures, commonly known as TERPS. In theory, keeping within TERPS guidelines keeps us safe. But the TERPS criteria for Category D aircraft said we could circle down to 2 statute miles visibility while using 2.3 nautical miles to maneuver. How could we keep an eye on the runway when it took more room to maneuver than the allowed visibility? Looking at my notes there was another problem. The units: 2.3 nautical miles comes to 2.65 statute miles. The odds were stacked against us from the start.

"Well I guess that explains a lot," Steve said after studying my notes. "Never trust the F of AA. You ought to write a training guide, Eddie. It would help us instructors and it might start a trend."

"Trend?" I half said, half asked.

"Yeah, it would be our very first training guide," he said. "We got to start somewhere."

The next week Captain Steve Kowalski became Major Steve Kowalski and I became the squadron's only captain pilot. The week after that Captain Russell DeLeon showed up from training to keep me company.

"The boss was pretty unhappy with me," he said, grinning. "I guess he doesn't like it when guys don't get their ATPs."

"Santelli?" I asked.

"Yeah," he said. "What does it take to get trained around here?"

"You got to be friends with that guy," I said, pointing to the scheduling office. Russell walked into Alton's talons, not ready for what was to come.

"Tell me this," Alton said to his catch of the day, "if you have a lake with a non-permeable shore and no means of adding or subtracting water, and if you were sitting in a boat, and if I were to happen by the shore and threw in a rock, would the level of the lake go up, go down, or stay the same?"

Russell hemmed and hawed and Alton was not amused. "Come on Einstein," he said, "if you're smart enough to fly a Boeing Friggin' 747 you ought to be able to figure this out."

"It would go up," Russell said.

"Very good," Alton said with an exaggerated glee, "you got that right. Now, what if I handed that rock to you in the boat?"

"I don't know," Russell said, "I don't know much about boats." He fled and Alton was suddenly without a victim.

"No use playing with you, *Ed-you-el*. Any engineer worth his salt knows this one."

"Yup," I said and returned to the only riddle I was interested in: circling approaches.

Circling Approaches

Approach Category

[14 CFR 97.3] Aircraft approach category means a grouping of aircraft based on a speed of V_{REF}, if specified, or if V_{REF} is not specified, $1.3V_{SO}$ at the maximum certificated weight. V_{SO}, and the maximum certificated landing weight are those values as established for the aircraft by the certification authority of the country of registry. These categories are as follows:

Category A: Speed less than 91 knots

Category B: Speed 91 knots or more but less than 121 knots

Category C: Speed 121 knots or more but less than 141 knots

Category D: Speed 141 knots or more but less than 166 knots

Category E: Speed 166 knots or more

[ICAO Doc 8168 PANS-OPS Vol 1, §4, ¶1.3]

The criterion taken into consideration for the classification of aeroplanes by categories is the indicated airspeed at threshold (Vat), which is equal to the stall speed Vso multiplied by 1.3, or stall speed Vs1g multiplied by 1.23 in the landing configuration at the maximum certificated landing mass. If both Vso and Vs1g are available, the higher resulting Vat shall be applied.

The landing configuration that is to be taken into consideration shall be defined by the operator or by the aeroplane manufacturer.

Aircraft categories will be referred to throughout this document by their letter designations as follows:

Category A: less than 169 km/h (91 kt) indicated airspeed (IAS)

Category B: 169 km/h (91 kt) or more but less than 224 km/h (121 kt) IAS

Category C: 224 km/h (121 kt) or more but less than 261 km/h (141 kt) IAS

Category D: 261 km/h (141 kt) or more but less than 307 km/h (166 kt) IAS

Category E: 307 km/h (166 kt) or more but less than 391 km/h (211 kt) IAS

Category H: see 1.3.10, "Helicopters".

These speeds are the same as used in the United States but the criteria is slightly different. If you have a V_{SO} and a V_{SIG} for your aircraft, you must use the higher of V_{SO} times 1.3 or V_{SIG} times 1.23.

Circling Approach Area [AIM fig 5-4-28]

In 2009 TERPS was changed to expand the circling approach maneuvering radius but left the old criteria in place for approaches already designed.

STANDARD CIRCLING APPROACH MANEUVERING RADIUS

Circling approach protected areas developed prior to late 2012 used the radius distances shown in the following table, expressed in nautical miles (NM), dependent on aircraft approach category. The approaches using standard circling approach areas can be identified by the absence of the **C** symbol on the circling line of minima.

Circling MDA in feet MSL	Approach Category and Circling Radius (NM)				
	CAT A	CAT B	CAT C	CAT D	CAT E
All Altitudes	1.3	1.5	1.7	2.3	4.5

C EXPANDED CIRCLING APPROACH MANEUVERING AIRSPACE RADIUS

Circling approach protected areas developed after late 2012 use the radius distance shown in the following table, expressed in nautical miles (NM), dependent on aircraft approach category, and the altitude of the circling MDA, which accounts for true airspeed increase with altitude. The approaches using expanded circling approach areas can be identified by the presence of the **C** symbol on the circling line of minima.

Circling MDA in feet MSL	Approach Category and Circling Radius (NM)				
	CAT A	CAT B	CAT C	CAT D	CAT E
1000 or less	1.3	1.7	2.7	3.6	4.5
1001-3000	1.3	1.8	2.8	3.7	4.6
3001-5000	1.3	1.8	2.9	3.8	4.8
5001-7000	1.3	1.9	3.0	4.0	5.0
7001-9000	1.4	2.0	3.2	4.2	5.3
9001 and above	1.4	2.1	3.3	4.4	5.5

[ICAO Doc 8168 Vol 1 PANS OPS] ICAO Radii are much larger:

Table I-4-7-1. Example of determining radii for visual manoeuvring (circling) area for aerodromes at 300 m MSL (SI units)

Category of aircraft/IAS (km/h)	A/185	B/250	C/335	D/380	E/445
TAS at 600 m MSL + 46 km/h wind factor (km/h)	241	310	404	448	516
Radius (r) of turn (km)	1.28	2.08	3.46	4.34	5.76
Straight segment (km)	0.56	0.74	0.93	1.11	1.30
Radius (R) from threshold (km)	3.12	4.90	7.85	9.79	12.82

Table I-4-7-2. Example of determining radii for visual manoeuvring (circling) area for aerodromes at 1 000 ft MSL (non-SI units)

Category of aircraft/IAS (kt)	A/100	B/135	C/180	D/205	E/240
TAS at 2 000 ft MSL + 25 kt wind factor (kt)	131	168	215	242	279
Radius (r) of turn (NM)	0.69	1.13	1.85	2.34	3.12
Straight segment (NM) (this is a constant value)	0.30	0.40	0.50	0.60	0.70
Radius (R) from threshold (NM)	1.68	2.66	4.20	5.28	6.94

Obstacle Clearance Surface (OCS), Required Obstacle Clearance (ROC)

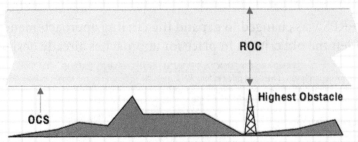

[TERPS 202.] Level OCS. The level OCS concept is applicable to "level flight" segments. These segments are level flight operations intended for en route, initial, intermediate segments, and nonprecision final approaches. A single ROC value is applied over the length of the segment. These values were determined through testing and observation of aircraft and pilot performance in various flight conditions. Typical ROC values are: for en route procedure segments, 1,000 feet (2,000 over designated mountainous terrain); and for initial segments, 1,000 feet, 500 feet in intermediate segments, and 350/300/250 feet in final segments.

[TERPS 260b.] Provide 300 ft Required Obstacle Clearance plus adjustments over the highest obstacle in the Obstacle Evaluation Area.

[ICAO Doc 8168 Vol 1, Figure I-4-1-4] Visual Manoeuvring (Circling). The Obstacle Clearance Height shall not be less than:

Category A 120 m (394 ft)

Category B 150 m (492 ft)

Category C 180 m (591 ft)

Category D 210 m (689 ft)

Category E 240 m (787 ft)

Minimum Obstacle Clearance (MOC)

Category A & B 90 m (295 ft)

Category C & D 120 m (394 ft)

Category E 150 m (492 ft)

Note: MOC may include an additional margin in mountainous terrain and is increased for remote and forecast altimeter settings.

Maneuvering

Determine the Drift. While you are on the instrument approach course prior to commencing your circle, make note of the drift required to maintain course. The heading offset needed will be important when you set up on downwind.

Offset Heading and Timing. The techniques that follow are easiest at cardinal speeds: 120 and 150 knots for example:

$r = (nm/min)^2 / 10$

At 120 knots (2 nm/min), r = 0.4 nm

At 150 knots (2-1/2 nm/min), r = 0.625 nm

Approach 90° to Runway

Time to delay downwind turn is the distance divided by the velocity. At 150 knots, for example:

$$t = \frac{0.625}{150} \times 3600 = 15 \text{ seconds}$$

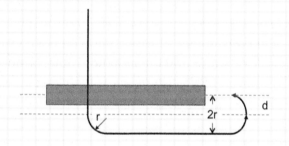

Approach From Opposite Runway

The distance traveled "d" on a 30° offset is twice the turn radius divided by the sine of 30°. For 150 knots, that comes to (2)(0.625)/sine(30) = 2.5nm. The time to fly that leg is the distance divided by the speed 2.5 / (150 x 60) = 60 seconds.

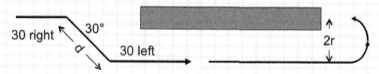

Rules of Thumb

To provide circling offset when approaching a runway at 90°, overfly the runway and time for 15 seconds (Category D) / 20 seconds (Category C) before turning downwind. To provide offset when approaching from the opposite runway, turn 30° away from heading, time for 60 seconds (Category D) / 70 seconds (Category C), and then turn downwind.

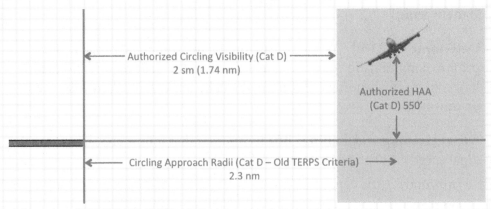

Adjusting TERPS Visibility Minimums

Note that the TERPS circling approach radii (based on nautical miles) which exceed the minimum visibilities (based on statute miles). This means you can easily lose sight of the runway if your maneuvering is based on the full radii. Older TERPS criteria do not consider the effects of pressure altitude or winds and often do not allow for normal maneuvering bank angles. Neither TERPS criteria allow for a long enough distance on final to provide a stable approach. A true minimum visibility would consider the following:

	Category C	Category D
Maximum circling speed (kts)	140	165
Final approach length (nm) for a stablized approach beginning not less than 500 ft. above the runway	1.4	1.4
Turn diameter buffer (nm)	+1.2	+1.7
Wind buffer (nm)	+0.5	+0.5
Total (nm)	3.1	3.6
Total (sm)	3.6	4.2
Recommended minimum visibility	3.6	4.2

Circling at less than these minimums will risk losing sight of the runway when maneuvering and will not provide the opportunity for a stabilized approach beginning at 500 feet above the runway.

18: Eruption

KC-135A Air Refueling an E-4B (USAF Photo)

On January 20, 1989, President Ronald Reagan's second term came to an end and with it our trips to California became trips to New Hampshire, near enough to the new president's cabin at Walker's Point, Maine. As if on cue, the Air Force dropped a hammer on all majors vying for promotion the second time around. Not a single major in the squadron was promoted. Major Tom Polanshek got picked up by Northwest Airlines and was gone in less than a month. Major Mark Thomas followed him out the door, on his way to American Airlines. Only Greg White stayed behind. His last act before unemployment was to administer my check ride for upgrade to aircraft commander.

"Pretty good, Eddie," he said after signing the paperwork. "Make sure you get into the training section as soon as possible. The squadron uses aircraft commanders to keep Whamo happy. The real fun is reserved for instructors."

My next month was consumed by the guys in the office behind the vaulted door, learning three new code words to go along with the Patriot Blue clearance I already had. I was almost always gone on a trip as the squadron traded lieutenant colonels for majors and majors for captains. The new cadre of pilots cut their teeth without me. I heard from the grapevine the new generation was filled with complaints about the training program and for the first time in anyone's memory, our squadron was busting new copilots and navigators. Once all the newbies were upgraded, it was finally time for me to upgrade to instructor pilot.

"Where's the training guide?" I asked.

"We don't got no stinking training guide," Major Kowalski said. "You know that."

"We should have a training guide," I said. "How else do we know what the training standard is?"

"Okay," he said. "You want a training guide, you write one." I wrote one. The rest of the Air Force was filled with training guides so I took one of those, folded in the United Airlines version, and made up the rest. I envisioned five training sorties to check off all the items I thought an instructor pilot should be able to demonstrate as well as the check ride standards. The act of writing an instructor's guide, I discovered, was the best way to learn the material. I presented my masterpiece to the squadron commander who approved it without even opening the front cover.

"I'm pretty busy right now, Eddie," Colonel Ellison said. "I'm sure it's fine. Tell the training department to start using it right away."

Each of my training sorties was easy. My instructors had to follow the brand new training guide; a training guide I knew from cover to cover, having just written it. Five sorties later I became an instructor pilot and camped out in the scheduling office waiting for my first sortie as a bona fide Boeing 747 instructor pilot. The board showed two copilots upgrading to aircraft commander and two new pilots just arriving from United Airlines. Both of the newbies had received their airline transport pilot licenses.

A knock at the door revealed the first of the new copilots.

"Higher," the pilot said in answer to Alton's "hand you the rock" question.

"Good," Alton said with his usual pretend glee, "now does the level of the lake go higher if I hand you the rock or if I throw the rock into the lake?"

"The lake," the pilot said, "it goes higher if you throw it in the lake because all of the rock is under water in that case."

"Wrong!" Alton chortled, "The level goes up by the same amount. Displacement is displacement! I guess I can't fault you because you aren't a genuine

Purdue graduate engineer like Captain *Ed-you-el* here."

The pilot shrugged his shoulders and took off. Alton sat back in his chair, satisfied with the belittle du jour. "Truth be known *Ed-you-el*," Alton said, "I graduated with a degree in English. But I like engineering just like I was the real thing."

"That explains it," I said.

"What?"

"You got it wrong. The lake goes higher when you hand the rock to the person in the boat than if you were to throw it in."

"No!" Alton said with even more joy, "I can't believe a real engineer doesn't know this. I guess we aren't getting what we pay for when we send one of our boys to Purdue these days."

"Displacement," I said, "is not displacement."

"Ah," Alton said and then fell silent. In a minute he recovered. "That isn't so." He spent the next hour arguing with me, even drawing a picture.

"When you throw the rock into the lake, the displacement is equal to the volume of the rock," I said. "When you hand the rock to the person in the boat, the displacement becomes the volume of the air inside the boat equal to the weight of the rock, a much higher figure because the air is less dense."

Alton looked as if I had shaken a religious tenet and I sat back, thinking of a gentle way to reveal the truth without shattering his core faith, but we were both interrupted.

"Eddie," Colonel Ellison said from the doorway, "we need you to investigate something. A 747 just flew through some volcanic ash in Alaska and lost all four engines. They got them restarted, but they almost lost the airplane. You need to get smart on this and teach us what to do if it ever happens to us."

I left Alton's office without another word and studied the report. The airplane was operated by KLM Airlines, a Dutch airline. They were at 25,000 feet when they wandered into what they thought was just a regular cloud. It didn't show up on radar and wasn't on any weather reports. There was a previous incident with a British Airways Boeing 747 in 1982. That airplane also lost all four engines until they exited the cloud. The airplane was heavily damaged.

The Boeing 747 was the world's premier long haul airplane and the airlines got into gear quickly to face this threat. The obvious solution was to avoid volcanic ash at all cost but we still had a long way to go with getting the information out to pilots. The engines quit because the ash became molten in the engine hot sections and then re-solidified in the turbine vanes, clogging the engine. Once the engines shut down and cooled, the solid ash became brittle and broke off, allowing the engines to be restarted.

I wrote new squadron procedures for "inadvertent volcanic ash encounter" and returned my focus to training pilots. But first I had a puzzle to complete.

I entered Alton's office with a small bucket, filled halfway with water, a ruler, a plastic cup, and a rock. "Look here Alton," I said while placing the pail on his desk. "We got exactly fifty millimeters of water with only the plastic cup on the surface."

"That you do," Alton said, a bit suspiciously.

"Now I will put the rock in the cup first so I don't remove any of the water trying to fish it out, okay?" He nodded. I placed the rock in the cup and we both saw the level rise. "What do you see there?"

"Looks like sixty-five," he said.

"Yup," I agreed, "I take the rock out of the cup and it returns to fifty." We both saw the level return. "Now if I drop the rock into the pail, according to your theory, it will go back to sixty-five. But if I am right, the level will be less than that. Right?" He nodded again.

I dropped the rock and the level barely moved, maybe reaching fifty-three.

"Well I'll be," he said, "I've been using that puzzle for ten years and I was wrong. You know what this means *Ed-you-el*?"

"You owe me an apology?" I guessed.

"No," he said. "It means the guy who gave me the puzzle didn't know what he was talking about. And that guy is going to be our new squadron commander."

I looked at the scheduling board. Lieutenant Colonel Ellison was retiring after 20 years, on his way to becoming a FedEx pilot. The new guy was Lieutenant Colonel Rodney G. Larson.

"Rodney?" I asked.

"Lieutenant Colonel Larson to you," Alton said. "You watch yourself, *Ed-you-el*. Larson is one of those career types shooting for promotion. He was a pain in the ass as a squadron pilot and stabbed everyone in the back to get his headquarter's job. His plan all along was to get back here as the boss and to use this squadron on his way to general officer's stars. Rodney G. Larson's top priority is Rodney G. Larson. And Rodney G. Larson doesn't like boat rockers."

"But I'm not," I started to say but stopped. "Maybe I am."

Volcanic Ash Avoidance and Recovery

A Few Sound Ideas:

- When in doubt, don't fly.

- Use available resources for forecasts and reports.

- Identify the location of both ash and clear areas.

- Keep your focus on what you are doing.

The Threat

[ICAO Doc 9691, ¶4.1] Volcanic ash is mostly glass shards and pulverized rock, very abrasive and, being largely composed of siliceous materials, with a melting temperature below the operating temperature of jet engines at cruise thrust. The ash is accompanied by gaseous solutions of sulphur dioxide (sulphuric acid) and chlorine (hydrochloric acid).

[ICAO Doc 9691, ¶2.3.1] One of the prime means of recognizing that an aircraft has encountered volcanic ash is the static electricity discharge exhibited by St. Elmo's fire on the airframe and the glow inside the jet engines. The static electric charge on the aircraft also creates a "cocoon" effect which may cause a temporary deterioration, or even complete loss, of VHF or HF communications.

[ICAO Doc 9691, ¶4.2]

- Volcanic ash has a melting point below jet engine operating temperatures with thrust settings above idle. The ash melts in the hot section of the engine and fuses on the high pressure nozzle guide vanes and turbine blades. This drastically reduces the high pressure turbine inlet guide-vane throat area causing the static burner pressure and compressor discharge pressure to increase rapidly which, in turn, causes engine surge. This effect alone can cause immediate thrust loss and possible engine flame-out.

- The sudden thermal and pressure shocks of the ram air during the restart process, coupled with the cooling of the fused ash deposit when the engine is reduced to idle, seem to break off much of the deposit. Moreover, subsequent operation of the engines after restart, in the clearer air outside the ash cloud, also seems to further dislodge and evacuate some of the fused ash deposits.

- The volcanic ash being abrasive also erodes compressor rotor paths and rotor blade tips (mostly high pressure section), causing loss of high pressure turbine efficiency and engine thrust. The erosion also results in a decrease in the engine stall margin.

- In addition to the melting/fusing of the volcanic ash and the blade erosion problems referred to above, the ash can clog flow holes in the fuel and cooling systems, although these particular effects appear to be rather variable.

Ash Encounter Indicators

[ICAO Doc 9974, ¶1.3 and 1.4]

- In day visual meteorological conditions (VMC) a precursor to a volcanic ash encounter will likely be a visual indication of a volcanic ash cloud or haze. If a flight crew observes a cloud or haze suspected of containing volcanic ash they should be aware that a volcanic ash encounter is imminent and they should take action to avoid the contaminated airspace.

- Odour. When encountering volcanic ash, flight crews usually notice a smoky or acrid odour that can smell like electrical smoke or sulphur.

- Haze. Most flight crews, as well as passengers, see a haze develop within the aircraft cockpit and/or cabin. Dust can settle on surfaces.

- Changing engine conditions. Surging, torching from the tailpipe, and flameouts can occur. Engine temperatures can change unexpectedly, and a white glow can appear at the engine inlet.

- Airspeed. If volcanic ash fouls the pitot tube, the indicated airspeed can decrease or fluctuate erratically.

- Pressurization. Cabin pressure can change, including possible loss of cabin pressurization.

- Static discharges. A phenomenon similar to St. Elmo's fire or glow can occur. In these instances, blue-coloured sparks can appear to flow up the outside of the windshield or a white glow can appear at the leading edges of the wings or at the front of the engine inlets.

- Any of these indicators should suffice to alert the flight crew of an ash encounter, and appropriate action should be taken to vacate the contaminated airspace as safely and expeditiously as possible.

Procedures

[ICAO Doc 9691, ¶4.4]

- Immediately reduce thrust to idle. This will lower the exhaust-gas temperature, which in turn will reduce the fused ash build-up on the turbine blades and hot-section components.

- Turn autothrottles off (if engaged) to prevent the thrust from increasing.

- Exit volcanic ash cloud as quickly as possible. Volcanic ash may extend for several hundred miles. The shortest distance/time out of the ash may require an immediate, descending 180-degree turn, terrain permitting. Attempting to climb above the volcanic ash cloud is not recommended due to accelerated engine damage/flame-out at high thrust settings.

- Turn engine and wing anti-ice and all air conditioning packs on. This will further improve the engine stall margin by increasing the bleed-air flow. It may be possible to stabilize one or more engines at the idle thrust setting where the EGT will remain within limits.

- Start the auxiliary power unit (APU), if available. The APU can be used to power the electrical system in the event of a multiple- engine power loss. The APU may also provide a pneumatic air source for improved engine starting, depending on the aircraft model.

- Put oxygen mask on at 100 percent, if required. Manual deployment of passenger oxygen masks is not recommended if cabin pressure is normal because the passenger oxygen supply will be diluted with volcanic ash.

- Restart engines. If an engine fails to start, try again immediately. Successful engine start may not be possible until airspeed and altitude are within the air-start envelope. Monitor EGT carefully.

- Monitor airspeed and pitch attitude. If unreliable, or if a complete loss of airspeed indication occurs, establish the appropriate pitch attitude dictated by the operations manual for "flight with unreliable airspeed."

- Land at the nearest suitable airport. A precautionary landing should be made at the nearest suitable airport if aircraft damage or abnormal engine operation occurs due to volcanic ash penetration.

- Volcanic ash on windshields and landing lights may reduce visibility for approach and landing. Diversion to an airport where an autolanding can be accomplished should be considered.

19: Going the Distance

E-4B Awaits Crew (Adrian Vargo)

As members of the 1st Airborne Command Control Squadron we were part of Offutt Air Force Base and the 55th Reconnaissance Wing for administrative purposes, such as the change of command ritual between outgoing and incoming squadron commanders. Most of the squadron would spend the morning in dress blues as the wing commander administered the oath of office to our new boss, Lieutenant Colonel Rodney Larson.

I would miss the fun because I was operational with the call sign "Gordo Four" flying a mission the wing commander knew nothing about. We had a cover story invented purely for the purpose of keeping him from going insane when thinking that the biggest, most expensive operation on his turf was completely outside of his purview.

I was happy to be in my office chair, the one that sat on the third floor of our 800,000 pound jet. "We ready?" I asked the flight engineer.

"Sections report in," Pete said over the aircraft-wide intercom.

"Communications ready," the first report came in. "Wire ready." "Crew chiefs ready." "Security ready." Finally, from the lead flight attendant, "passengers seated and galley is ready."

"All set," I heard from Mark Honable, seated at the navigator's table.

"We be ready," Pete said.

"Let's go," I said. "Start 'em up."

Pete and Major Keith Rawlings, our newest copilot, started the engines and ran the before taxi checklist as I pondered my options. The visibility was down to 500 feet in thick, dense fog. Flying a Whamo mission gave me the authority to waive all Air Force minimums and doing so in muck down to 500 feet would certainly not be unusual. I was more worried about loose objects on the taxiways or perhaps a ground vehicle that had lost its way onto the runway. There wasn't much I could do about that.

"Ready for taxi," Pete said.

"Okay then," I said. "Everyone eyes outside please, I'm going to take my time."

I inched the airplane to the wrong side of the runway, knowing it would be easier to taxi on the deserted runway and do a 180 degree turn, than to negotiate the winding parallel taxiway to the correct side. But even on the runway I had to take it slow.

"Pilot, nav," Honable said.

"Go," I said.

"Alpha wants to talk to you," he said.

"Tell him I'm busy," I said.

"I'm not telling him that," Mark said.

I flicked my eyes from the runway centerline to the interphone panel on my left and punched at the button I knew held the command post frequency. "This is Gordo Four pilot."

"This is alpha," the wing commander said, as if he was at the bar trading stories with his best friend. "I am sitting here on the parallel and I hear your engines but don't see you. Where are you?"

"Sir," I said, "we are back taxiing to the opposite end of the runway."

"What are you going to do when you get there," he asked. A ridiculous question.

"We are going to take off," I said. It was a reasonable answer, I thought. But the audible gasp from the rest of the crew told me I might have been wrong. "Sir," I added. He said nothing and we took off into the murky soup.

Later that day there was no sign of fog, the squadron had a new commander, and I lowered the aircraft onto the same runway where everything had begun ten hours earlier. I walked into the squadron and into the flight crew ready room, where the new commander was mixing with the troops.

"You must be Eddie," he said as I entered.

"Yes, sir," I said. "Sorry I missed your change of command."

"Duty calls," he said. "That's why we are here, after all." The crowd laughed nervously and I sat to attack my post mission paperwork. "Well I got my own paperwork to tackle," he said, and with that he was gone.

"You're not going to believe what's gone down around here," Steve Kowalski said in hushed tones. "Nobody's going to tell you in public, but you need to find out."

Kowalski left before I could corner him and the squadron was close to deserted before I finished. "See you tomorrow, Eddie," the commander said in his whiney, broken glass voice. "Don't stay too late Alton."

Alton waved goodbye and sat in his chair until we both heard the door shut behind Colonel Larson. "*Ed-you-el*," he said while lowering himself into the seat opposite mine, "not everyone gets your sense of humor and you can bet Rodney Larson has no sense of humor at all."

"I guess I need the story from the opening verse," I said. "I really have no idea what is going on."

"Well it all began with your words to the wing king," he said. "In the normal world of the wing commander, his crews aren't allowed to take off in weather less than 1200 feet without a waiver from higher headquarters and that has to go through him."

"But," I started.

"But," he interrupted, "the powers that be in Washington, D.C. have bestowed that power on you, the humble E-4B aircraft commander. But the wing king forgot that and you didn't remind him. I had a good chuckle when I heard what you said. 'We're going to take off.' *Ed-you-el*, that's pretty funny. But not to a colonel who thinks one of his pilots is doing something reckless."

"I suppose," I said. "But if he objected he could have asked."

"Well he did ask," Alton said. "He asked the brand new squadron commander right after he handed him the keys to the squadron. Rodney promised your head on a platter, said he would personally chop it right off your scrawny shoulders. He came back to the squadron, breathing fire. It took us most the morning to calm him down and remind him that you were completely within the regulations."

"So now he looks stupid," I said.

"And now he has a problem," Alton said. "What is he to do with an instructor pilot that has done nothing technically wrong but whose head he promised to deliver to his boss?"

"That is a problem," I admitted.

"Well I got you on the mother of all trips on Monday," he said. "I figure if you disappear for a week things might cool off a bit."

The next trip was from Washington, D.C. to Tokyo, Japan, a mere trip of 5,889 nautical miles made mere by the presence of a KC-10 tanker waiting atop Alaska with 80,000 pounds of fuel destined for our thirsty engines. We could make the trip without the tanker, but just barely. The tanker made things easy, until it made things hard.

"Gordo Four," the tanker announced as we pulled within a few miles, "we got a problem."

"And what would that problem be?" I asked.

"Our boom is stuck," he said. "We've tried everything and it won't budge. Now we've got an extra 80,000 pounds of gas we don't know what to do with and I suppose you guys aren't going to make your destination."

"Okay," I said. "Good luck with the boom, we'll sort things out on this end."

"Can we make Japan?" I asked, to nobody in particular.

"The flight plan says we need 155,000," the engineer said, "all we got is 150."

"But the flight plan is at the higher weight," the copilot said. "We'll burn less because we weigh less."

"Not that much less," the engineer said. "Let me get the charts."

The engineer chased the lines on his fuel endurance charts and came up with 135,000. "Enough to make it," he said, "but not legally. We need at least 25 in reserve. We are 10 short."

"What if we pull it back?" the copilot asked.

"Flying more hours isn't going to help," the engineer said.

"It will," I said. "If we gradually bring the speed down to keep at maximum range speed, it might work. Meanwhile, let's point the nose to Japan and figure a point where we have to reverse course to get back to Alaska. Nav, go downstairs and visit the lead Whamo guy. Tell him we are going to be late."

Ten minutes later the engineer announced his conclusion. "Might work," he said, handing the charts and his computations to the copilot. Five minutes after that they handed it all to me. A minute later the decision was made. Five hours later we landed in Tokyo with 25,000 pounds of fuel in reserve.

Being halfway around the world was a good opportunity to unplug from the squadron except for a navigator who spent most of his en route time on the phone with Alton or anyone else who would answer.

"Congratulations, Eddie," he said.

"Why?" I asked.

"You just got promoted to major and they are making you the squadron test pilot," he said.

"The squadron doesn't have a test pilot," I said, "and everyone in our squadron makes major."

"Well, not everyone gets a school slot," he said. "In fact, you are the only one in the wing. Imagine that, out of sixty captains promoted to major, you are the only one nominated for school."

On my next break from the cockpit I took a trip downstairs and made a few phone calls of my own. The wing's promotion rate to major was pretty good, about seventy percent. Of those, five percent should have been nominated for school. There should have been three of us, not just one. Getting nominated wasn't the same as being selected, however. Only a quarter of those nominated would be selected, but all of those who made it to school were guaranteed promotion to lieutenant colonel.

"Where are you going?" I said to Kowalski via the satellite phone patch.

"Air Force One is getting their own 747," he said. "They want me to fly it. So you got the functional check pilot job. Larson was against it, but I told him you were the only one who wouldn't muck it up. He had no choice."

It seemed I was repeating a pattern from Hawaii. I made the long struggle from copilot, to aircraft commander, and finally to instructor pilot. Then, right after realizing the goal, I was diverted into something different. Since the Air Force only had four Boeing 747s our squadron was responsible for providing a pilot to perform functional check flights. These were not test flights; merely flights to verify the aircraft was performing to standards following heavy maintenance or modification. It wasn't the right stuff of Hollywood, but it was a good job nonetheless.

"So when do I get trained?" I asked.

"You don't need any training," he said. "I've seen you fly. You can do this."

"Okay," I said. "So how do I do this?"

"You tell me," he said. And with that, the phone went dead.

Steve was gone within the month. It took me another month to write a functional check pilot manual and I spent the next year flying broken and recently repaired Boeing 747s. It was great.

Range Performance

Range Versus Endurance

Some aeronautical textbooks can be misleading on the subject of range versus endurance because the aviation world changed with the jet engine. Prior to turbojets, many aeronautical texts considered range and endurance to be the same. This is true for a conventional reciprocating engine with a propeller. With a jet engine, however, flying at L/D_{MAX} gets you maximum endurance. If you want maximum range, you will need to fly faster than L/D_{MAX}.

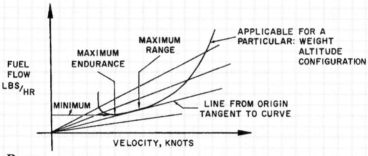

Specific Range

[ATCM 51-3, pg. 158] The problem of efficient range operation of an airplane appears in two general forms in flying operations: (1) to extract the maximum flying distance from a given fuel load or (2) to fly a specified distance with minimum expenditure of fuel. An obvious common denominator for each of these operating problems is the "specific range," nautical miles of flying distance per lb. of fuel.

$$\text{specific range} = \frac{\text{velocity, knots}}{\text{fuel flow, pounds per hour}}$$

If maximum specific range is desired, the flight condition must provide a maximum of velocity/fuel flow. This particular point would be located by drawing a straight line from the origin tangent to the curve of fuel flow versus velocity.

Notice on the chart that maximum endurance occurs when fuel flow is at a minimum. This is also L/D_{MAX}, which many aircraft will find at 0.3 angle of attack. Notice also on the chart that maximum range occurs at some point with higher fuel flow and a higher velocity. This is useful, of course, but how much higher? The answer can be found using trigonometry on the specific range chart; but in practice it is usually found through flight tests.

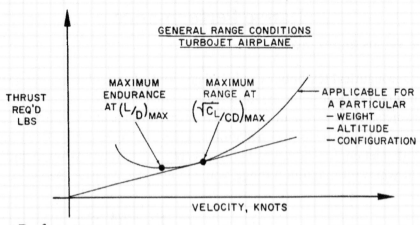

Range Performance

[ATCM 51-3, pg. 164] In the case of a turbojet airplane, the fuel flow is determined mainly by the thrust rather than power.

Thus, the fuel flow could be most directly related to the thrust required to maintain the airplane in steady, level flight. This fact allows study of the turbojet powered airplane by analysis of the curves of thrust required versus velocity. [The figure] illustrates a typical curve of thrust required versus velocity which would be (somewhat) analogous to the variation of fuel flow versus velocity. The maximum endurance condition would be obtained at $(L/D)_{MAX}$ since this would incur the lowest fuel flow to keep the airplane in steady, level flight. The maximum range condition would occur where the proportion between the velocity and thrust required is greatest and this point is located by drawing a straight line from the origin to the curve.

The maximum range is obtained at the aerodynamic condition which produces a maximum proportion between the square root of the lift coefficient (CL) and the drag coefficient (CD), or $(\sqrt{CL}/CD)_{MAX}$. In subsonic performance, $(\sqrt{CL}/CD)_{MAX}$ occurs at a particular value angle of attack and lift coefficient and is unaffected by weight or altitude (within compressibility limits). [The AOA is unaffected by weight or altitude; the velocity is greatly affected.] At this specific aerodynamic condition, induced drag is approximately 25 percent of total drag so the turbojet airplane designed for long range does not have the strong preference for a high aspect ratio planform like the propeller airplane. On the other hand, since approximately 75 percent of total drag is parasite drag, the turbojet airplane designed specifically for long range has the special requirement for great aerodynamic cleanness.

Effect of Gross Weight

[ATCM 51-3, pg. 164] The flight condition of ($\sqrt{CL}/CD$)$_{MAX}$ is achieved at one value of lift coefficient for a given airplane in subsonic flight. Hence, a vari-

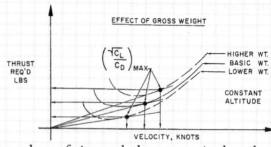

ation of gross weight will alter the values of airspeed, thrust required, and specific range obtained at ($\sqrt{CL}/CD$)$_{MAX}$.

All this means to the pilot is this: if you want to maintain maximum range while burning off fuel, your airspeed is going to have to come back. That in turn will decrease your required thrust setting while increasing your specific range. Alternatively, you can consider climbing.

Effect of Altitude

[ATCM 51-3, pg. 166] The effect of altitude on the range of the turbojet airplane is of great importance because no other single item can cause such large variations of specific range.

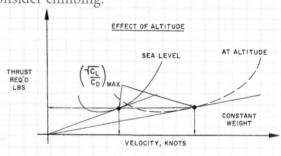

Notice that the entire thrust required curve shifts up and to the right with an increase in altitude.

An increase in altitude will improve powerplant performance in two respects. First, an increase in altitude when below the tropopause will provide lower inlet air temperatures which reduce the specific fuel consumption. Of course, above the tropopause the specific fuel consumption tends to increase. Thus a second benefit of altitude on engine performance is due to the increased RPM required to furnish cruise thrust. An increase in engine speed to the normal rated value will reduce the specific fuel consumption.

Most jet engines are more efficient at higher RPM's, you will get better range operating near the engine's RPM limits. Planning to operate at the upper limit of the airplane's cruise capability, however, poses a danger if the outside air temperature rises.

Endurance Performance

[ATCM 51-3, pg. 172] Since the fuel flow of the turbojet powered airplane is proportional to thrust required, the turbojet airplane will achieve maximum specific endurance when operated at minimum thrust required or $(L/D)_{MAX}$. In subsonic flight, $(L/D)_{MAX}$ occurs at a specific value of lift coefficient for a given airplane and is essentially independent of weight or altitude.

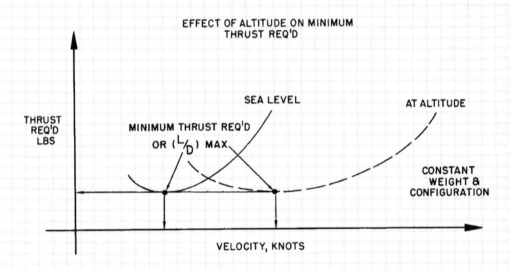

The specific fuel consumption of the turbojet engine is strongly affected by operating RPM and altitude. Generally, the turbojet engine prefers the operating range near normal rated engine speed and the low temperatures of the stratosphere to produce low specific fuel consumption. Thus, increased altitude provides the favorable lower inlet air temperature and requires a greater engine speed to provide the thrust required at $(L/D)_{MAX}$. The typical turbojet airplane experiences an increase in specific endurance with altitude with the peak values occurring at or near the tropopause.

Your best endurance occurs at the bottom of the tropopause (minimum temperature) and at the lower thrust settings needed to achieve L/D_{MAX} speeds.

Range Economy

Maximum range speed theoretically gets you from Point A to Point B with the most fuel remaining, but not necessarily at the lowest cost. As fuel prices go up, it becomes more critical to fly the aircraft at a lower average fuel consumption. As fuel prices drop, other variable costs become more imporant. If airplane maintenance and crew costs are charged by the hour, they can eventually overtake the influence of fuel economy.

Some modern flight management systems, particularly those in airline cock-pits, are adapted to consider these costs. A Boeing 737 flown by an airline may find it advantageous to fly faster in a headwind, because it costs more to pay the crew for added flight time than it does to pay for the fuel. Another airplane, flown without this additional hourly cost, could be flown just as economically at a slower speed.

Generally speaking, it only makes sense to discount the importance of fuel costs when other hourly variables start to exceed fuel costs. The following formula will help illustrate the trade off:

$$\text{Total Cost} = \left(\frac{D}{TAS - WF} \right) \times \left(FF \left(\frac{FC}{FD} \right) + VA + VC + VE \right)$$

FF — Fuel Flow (pounds per hour), average in cruise

FC — Fuel Cost ($ per gallon)

FD — Fuel Density (pounds per gallon)

D — Distance to cruise (since the climb and descent fuel will be about the same, we consider only the cruise portion)

TAS — True Air Speed during cruise

VA — Variable Airframe costs ($ per hour)

VC — Variable Crew costs ($ per hour)

VE — Variable Engine costs ($ per hour)

WF — Wind Factor (positive numbers for headwinds, negative for tailwinds)

If your cruise speed is determined by Mach number, you will need to convert that to knots True Air Speed (TAS) first. You will first need to determine the speed of sound:

Speed of Sound (When above 36,089' on an ISA day) = 573 nm/hr

Speed of Sound (When at or below 36,089' on an ISA day):

$$\textbf{Speed of Sound} = \textbf{29.06} \sqrt{\textbf{518.7} - \frac{\textbf{3.57 Altitude}}{\textbf{1000}}}$$

You can find TAS by dividing the Mach Number by the speed of sound:

$$\textbf{TAS} = \frac{\textbf{Mach}}{\textbf{Speed of Sound}}$$

G450 Example

If you consider a G450 cruising at 37,000 feet in a 100 knot headwind at 70,000 pounds and ISA, average fuel flow will be 2,966 PPH (M 0.77), 3,178 PPH (M 0.80), and 3,593 PPH (M 0.83). If the fuel costs $3 per gallon and has a density of 6.5 pounds per gallon, and the variable costs are as shown:

Mach	No Variable Costs	$1,000 Variable Costs	$3,000 Variable Costs
M 0.77	$12,035	$20,828	$38,413
M 0.80	$12,278	$20,648	$37,389
M 0.83	$13,245	$21,233	$37,207

As fuel costs drop, other variable costs become increasingly important. In the example shown it doesn't make sense to speed up in a headwind when there are no other variable costs. That makes sense, the faster you go the more fuel you burn. But as variable costs other than fuel increase, there comes a point where it pays to speed up because fuel would be cheaper than the other variable costs. Let's say you paid your crew by the hour and had a maintenance program billable by the hour. If those variable costs came to $3,000 per hour you'd be better off speeding up, as shown.

20: Dysfunctional

Haskel landing after a Functional Check Flight, 4/14/1991 (USAF Photo)

"Major Haskel," the squadron public address blared, "report to the commander's office." I dropped the half-eaten jelly donut back onto its plate and headed for Lieutenant Colonel Larson's office.

"Sir?" I said, peeking through the half-closed door.

"Eddie," he said, "come on in. I thought I would give you a pep talk about Air Command and Staff College."

"I'm not volunteering," I said. "I didn't submit the paperwork."

"Nonsense!" he said. "Of course you're volunteering. Not only that, you are going to be selected. Don't you realize how good this will make the squadron look? Don't you want to do this for us?"

"Not really," I said.

"Pretty funny!" he said. "I'm glad we had this talk, Eddie! Well, I know you are pretty busy with the upcoming test flights. Fly safe, Eddie!"

"Functional check flights," I said. "They aren't test flights."

"Pretty funny!" he said.

Our four Boeing 747s were a mixed bag of airplanes somehow engineered to be identical. The first two were originally built for Qantas Airlines to Australian specifications. A week before the final coat of paint and the Kangaroo logo decals were to go on, Qantas ran out of money. Boeing made the Air Force an offer they couldn't refuse. A few years later we bought a third airplane and made it like the first two. A few years after that, just before the 747-200 production line came to a close, airplane number four rolled onto our ramp.

Airplane number three was the problem child. As airplanes go, no big airplane is nicer to land than the 747. Except for airplane number three. Or at least that was what everyone said. I wasn't so sure. I do know I hated air-refueling number three. As easy as the 747 is to land, it is difficult to air refuel. Even under the most benign conditions, placing an 800,000 pound airplane a few feet behind a tanker at 25,000 feet and several hundreds of miles per hour can be daunting. For most of our pilots, it was sometimes a joy and sometimes an ordeal. When somebody started an aircraft diary for each airplane, it became clear that more times than not the ordeal was in airplane number three.

It was the "Sick Bag Metric." How many passengers got sick during the air refueling? Airplane number three easily claimed more victims than the rest of the fleet combined. For most of our pilots the primary symptom was misdiagnosed as "pilot induced oscillations," a rapid up and down movement that alternated the pressure on your behind with that against your lap belts and shoulder harnesses. For me, it was simply a feeling of flying sideways. Armed with that newly quantified data (sick bags), we funded a month of test flights at a Boeing 747 repair plant in Texas.

"Test flight" was the wrong terminology. The Air Force really gave up on those years ago. It doesn't make sense to take an airplane into the sky with the outcome uncertain. That costs too much in terms of dollars and lives. The official term is "functional check flight." The experts would work on the airplane until they thought it airworthy and I would fly it to prove or disprove that fact.

For our sideways airplane I asked the squadron to provide their choice of copilot and navigator and I picked a flight engineer who could keep me out of trouble.

Chief Master Sergeant Terry Wilson was flying airplanes long before I was even born and knew the 747 from nose to tail. He tended to drink too much on the road and was known for getting air sick in the simulator, but in the airplane he was a rock.

"Terry," I asked after strolling through the aircraft's interior, "why is there a very large rock in the forward cargo compartment?"

"It's for my garden. I picked it up at a local garden supply. We can't get these back home."

Terry wanted that rock and it seemed to him the best place to store it was right on the airplane. I didn't have a problem with it, so long as it was secured so it wouldn't shift in flight and we knew how much it weighed.

"How the hell should I know how much it weighs?" he asked.

"Terry, we either need the exact weight or you need to take it off the airplane until our tests are done."

"Major," he said to me in a professorial tone, "your airplane will weigh at least six hundred thousand pounds during the test flight; my rock ain't gonna make any difference."

"Terry, it's gonna have to be like this." I was trying to avoid the major to sergeant lecture, but my odds were looking slim. "We have controllability issues and I want to rule out center of gravity as a variable. You either weigh the rock or you take it off the airplane."

"You know how many guys it took to get that thing on the airplane?" I said nothing. He took the rock off the airplane.

The Boeing engineer's first theory about our controllability issue was a misrigged aileron system. Every control surface on the 747 is hydraulically powered with no cable backups. The actuators were controlled by levers and pulleys, of course, but the forces were all a function of hydraulic piping diameters, pump forces, and artificial feel systems. Any link in that chain could have been at fault.

I brought the schematics to my hotel room, trying to formulate my questions for the next day's session with the Boeing technicians. I was deep into the flight control rigging manual when the phone on the generic nightstand rang.

"Eddie, it's Lieutenant Colonel Larson. We need you to submit a volunteer letter for school."

"I don't know that I want to go to Air Command and Staff College."

"If you don't volunteer," Larson insisted, "you ain't going. So you should at least volunteer, you can always turn it down."

Of course if I did that, I would be stealing someone else's opportunity. Air Command and Staff College, what we all called "colonel charm school," was a guarantee for promotion but also a good way to end a flying career. Getting promoted would be nice, but very few lieutenant colonels in the Air Force get to fly airplanes. "I'll think about it."

The next day I was only thinking about stall speeds.

"Okay guys," I said over the interphone system, "pre-stall checks are complete, I am hand flying the airplane at twenty-five thousand feet, the airplane weighs six-hundred, twenty-four thousand pounds, the air is calm, and the configuration is clean. I just need a target stall speed."

"Looks like about one-thirty." I could see copilot Dave Winters chasing through the airplane performance charts with the end of his index finger; not the kind of precision I was looking for.

"I don't want about, I want an exact number."

"But, Eddie." I stared at him and he stopped midsentence.

Stalling a Cessna 150 is something all student pilots learn to do so that they may forever avoid doing just that on larger aircraft. The only reason we were doing it on our considerably larger airplane was to validate its low speed flying characteristics. I had done it many times and the process was methodical. Because it was methodical, it was safe. I would decelerate the airplane at precisely two knots per second while keeping the wings level. The moment I felt a tremor in the controls, I knew the airflow over the wings was starting to separate. That would be the "stall onset" and Boeing provided data to predict exactly when that would happen. If it didn't happen or I somehow missed it, we would risk missing the stall onset and fly into the stall. As long as I kept the airplane in coordinated flight - no adverse yaw - the airplane would continue to fly. But since we had an airplane with controllability issues to begin with, we couldn't guarantee an adverse yaw free condition. Every pilot knows a stall plus adverse yaw equals a spin. And every 747 pilot knows a spin on an airplane this size is not survivable. We obviously couldn't risk that. We had to know at what point to abort the maneuver.

"One-thirty-one point five," he said.

"Good. Start timing. Pulling half a knob on two."

I pulled the two inboard throttles back about half a knob-width, about a half-inch. Dave read off the airspeed and it looked like about two knots per second. At 150 knots I felt a tremor in my left hand. It had to be a mistake. At 146 the tremor was a rumble.

"Onset at 146," I said while pushing the throttles forward slightly, "that can't be right."

We repeated the entry four times, each time with the same results. It was time to tear the airplane's flight controls apart.

After two days of looking into inspection panels, measuring hydraulic pressures, and testing individual control units, we had nothing. I alternated hours with the mechanics and technicians with phone calls from Lieutenant Colonel Larson.

"We need a highly qualified major from this squadron to volunteer for ACSC," he said with no sense of irony, "and I'm going to volunteer you."

"What about next year?"

"What about it?"

The next theory for our too-early stall was something pilots have known about for a while, but usually isn't a problem on the 747: spoiler blow up. We have several panels on the top of each wing that have three functions. First, they assist the airplane's ailerons when rolling the airplane left or right. In a right turn, for example, the right spoilers deflect upward, spoiling the lift on only one wing. The result is a crisper turn. On the ground all the spoilers go up and act as ground spoilers to help bring the airplane to a stop. In the air they can also be used together as speed brakes, to help the aircraft descend. During slow speed flight, the air on top of the wing becomes a vacuum that can suck the spoilers out of position, the so-called spoiler blow up. That would explain our too-early stall.

Since you can't see the wings from the cockpit of a 747, we got permission to put a company technician in a window seat next to each wing. "Tell me what the spoilers are doing," I said.

I snuck the throttles back and Dave called the airspeed decay. I felt the rumble. "Anything on the wings?" I asked over the interphone.

"Left wing, nothing, sir."

"Right wing, nothing, sir."

A few more knots. "Anything?"

Silence, and then, "spoiler deflection right!"

"What about left?"

"Nothing."

How can that be? I aborted the maneuver and ordered the observers to the cockpit. Perhaps the left wing technician didn't know what to look for. "Let's try it again, this time trade wings."

"Spoiler deflection right!"

"Left wing, nothing."

It didn't make sense. Why just one wing? I inched the throttles forward and kept the airspeed steady. The tremor in my left hand was now a constant buzz. I looked at my hand. I was holding the right wing down and the yoke was deflected a good thirty degrees. The spoiler on the right wing was deflected because I was telling it to deflect.

"Look at the ailerons."

"You're causing the deflection," Terry said. "Major, why are you doing that?"

"I'm keeping the wings level," I said, "I guess subconsciously to keep from yawing the aircraft. Of course I'm doing just the opposite."

I pushed the throttles forward a bit. "Let me think about it."

Something was causing the aircraft to roll left and I was counteracting that by raising my left hand to command an opposite roll. So maybe the spoilers aren't the issue at all.

"Okay," I said over interphone, "here's the plan. We'll enter the stall with the airplane in a thirty-degree bank to the right. I'll try to time the airspeed decay so that I can keep the ailerons flush until we've rolled into a thirty-degree bank to the left. We'll record that speed and call it a day."

We got it right on the first attempt. As the speed dipped below 150, I centered the aileron input and the airplane rolled slowly to the left. As the wings were parallel to the horizon the speed was about 140. At thirty degrees bank to the left we were at the precise stall speed and the tremor in the controls returned.

"The airplane is stalling at the correct speed," I announced, "but our real problem is an uncommanded roll at low speeds."

We were doing all our flying from an aircraft plant an hour east of Dallas, living in a filthy Holiday Inn, and eating most of our meals at a Burger King. The rest of the crew found ways to keep themselves diverted each night while I looked at schematics and argued with squadron mates over the phone on one topic or another.

It was an open-ended arrangement. We were stuck there until the airplane was fixed. After the second week I got a stack of mail that included an envelope from the Air Force personnel center. I had officially volunteered for Air Command and Staff College.

"But I don't want to go." I called Lieutenant Colonel Larson at his home.

"You didn't tell me that, in so many words."

"Well, that's what I meant."

"Don't worry about it, Eddie. The selection rate is less than one-half of one percent."

"It's a Q-spring on the top rudder," the plant's chief engineer announced, "we are certain of it."

After our fourth check flight and discovery of the roll problem, the aircraft was attacked by technicians and mechanics looking for anything that could cause an uncommanded roll. I remember learning about the Q-spring in school, but hadn't given it much thought ever since.

The rudder on the 747 is huge. Actually there are two, one on top and another below it. They are attached to the vertical fin and are connected to pedals at each pilot's feet. With a press of either pedal the pilot can induce a yawing moment to either assist the coordination of a turn or to align the aircraft with the runway on takeoff or landing. Because the rudders are so huge the hydraulic system provides nearly all the force necessary. As a result, the pilot is left with little or no feedback in his feet and as such, doesn't have a "feel" for what the rudders are doing.

The Q-spring on older Boeings is just that, a spring that gives the pilot a small measure of feedback. On the 747 it is a bit more complicated, but not much.

"The top Q-spring unit was actually seized into one piece so that it only deflects the rudder to the right," the engineer explained. "It would be hardly noticeable."

"Would it explain our issues during air refueling and landing?"

"I find that hard to believe," he answered. "But I'm not a pilot. I guess anything is possible."

In two days the entire top rudder actuator assembly, including the Q-spring unit, was replaced. The next day the airplane stalled completely normally. The day after that we ordered a tanker and had the time of our lives air refueling.

"This is easy," Dave said while inching the airplane forward for his second contact with the tanker, "I could do this for hours."

"Congratulations," the general officer on the phone said. When I heard the call was from Montgomery, Alabama I knew I should have been concerned. "You've been selected for next year's Air Command and Staff College."

Functional Check Flights (FCFs)

What an FCF is . . .

[Technical Order 1-1-300, ¶4.1] Check flights are performed to determine whether an aircraft and its various components are functioning according to predetermined specifications while subjected to the flight environment. Such flights are conducted when it is not feasible to determine safe or required operation (aerodynamic reaction, air loading, signal propagation, etc.) by means of ground or shop tests.

[14 CFR 91, § 91.407] Operation after maintenance, preventive maintenance, rebuilding, or alteration.

(a) No person may operate any aircraft that has undergone maintenance, preventive maintenance, rebuilding, or alteration unless—

(1) It has been approved for return to service by a person authorized under §43.7 of this chapter; and

(2) The maintenance record entry required by §43.9 or §43.11, as applicable, of this chapter has been made.

(b) No person may carry any person (other than crewmembers) in an aircraft that has been maintained, rebuilt, or altered in a manner that may have appreciably changed its flight characteristics or substantially affected its operation in flight until an appropriately rated pilot with at least a private pilot certificate flies the aircraft, makes an operational check of the maintenance performed or alteration made, and logs the flight in the aircraft records.

(c) The aircraft does not have to be flown as required by paragraph (b) of this section if, prior to flight, ground tests, inspection, or both show conclusively that the maintenance, preventive maintenance, rebuilding, or alteration has not appreciably changed the flight characteristics or substantially affected the flight operation of the aircraft.

What an FCF is not . . .

A functional check flight is not a "test flight" which requires FAA approval, tightly controlled protocols, and certain pilot qualifications. For more information, see 14 CFR 21 § 21.35.

FCF Risk Management

Is an FCF really necessary? First check to see if the test or data can be acquired on the ground. With today's computer driven aircraft, fewer flight tests are required than in the past. However, sometimes the only time a malfunction occurs is in flight and/or the only way to duplicate conditions is by putting the aircraft at altitude. Since there is no practical way to duplicate flight loads, aircraft structural flexing, temperatures and pressures on the ground, sometimes only a flight check will do.

Is it required by the maintenance manual? There are very few times when the maintenance manual requires a flight check. If a flight is required, specific checklists and procedures will/should be provided by the manufacturer.

In most cases a demonstration flight using normal procedures and a normal flight profile should suffice. If something beyond a strictly normal flight profile is required, carefully choose the FCF Crew. (See below.)

If the manufacturer will not provide a specific procedure and one is not available in the maintenance manual, an FCF procedure should be written well in advance and passed around to knowledgeable resources for critique.

The FCF sortie should be flown in good weather, day visual meteorological conditions and with easily understood rules and criteria for completion and abort.

Crew Selection

FCFs should be conducted with designated crew members that have the requisite competencies, skill sets and experience. This does not mean the pilots with the best hands, the most total time, or the most fearless personality. (A healthy fear and appropriate caution with a dash of skepticism is often best.) The crew should be technically inquisitive, knowledgeable of aircraft systems and their interrelationships, and restrictions. They should be skilled in observation, interpretation and analysis. FCFs require better risk evaluation, prioritization of tasks, a high level of teamwork and above all, integrity. Each member of the crew should tolerate delays well.

FCF Flight Preparation

The aircraft:

- What is the condition of the aircraft? Any MEL'd items or waivers?
- What were the disturbed systems? What areas of the aircraft were maintainers accessing? What systems were worked on? What parts were replaced or swapped?
- Were there any difficulties in the maintenance?
- What was the condition of the aircraft prior to maintenance?
- Were there any new maintenance procedures conducted?
- Are there any restrictions?
- Are the required documents on board?

The airfield:

- Are there any ground or flight restrictions/procedures dictated by the airport?
- Is fire coverage at primary and alternate airports sufficient?

The airspace:

- Coordinate with ATC for the airspace that you will need for the conduct of the flight. See if a particular time of day would be advantageous.
- See if there is a preferred route for a normal flight profile or a MOA or other air work area that would work best if you need to delay in an area or get an altitude block to safely conduct flight checks.

The weather:

- Daylight only.
- Ceiling and visibility criteria should be established based on the reason for the FCF. Most operators use basic VFR for all checks and higher (3500 / 3) for first flights or if avionics have been disturbed or are suspect. Criteria should be adjusted for any terrain or other peculiarities of the aerodrome.
- No icing or turbulence conditions. Gusts and crosswinds should have predetermined limits.
- No limiting runway conditions or contamination.

The FCF Sortie

CRM for an FCF is different than for a routine flight. The aircraft should be flown by a three man crew. The captain is the primary controls operator, responsible for the safety of the flight and is primary gatekeeper of the overall pacing, progress and conduct of the flight. The FO acts as communicator, systems operator, switch mover and works in concert with the captain and the third crewmember, the flight test engineer. The flight test engineer is a third pilot or maintenance technician that reads and runs the individual checks, takes copious notes and ensures that all required data is recorded and that the checks are conducted or aborted using the predetermined criteria. It is the engineer that sets the pacing of individual checklist items, ensuring that the aircraft has established the proper conditions and configurations.

The number of people onboard the aircraft should be restricted to the absolute minimum. If an additional person is not required for the checks to be performed, the three-person crew should be the only folks on board. Additional folks lead to crew distraction, divided attention and possible interference with the purpose of the flight.

The FCF Profile

- Fly a normal flight profile if at all possible. If there is not a compelling need for high speed / low speed handling characteristics or data recording, fly normal operational speeds. The same goes for altitude, bank angles, descent and climb rates, etc. Don't test for the sake of testing or just "seeing what it would do".

- Always stay within AFM limits.

- The flight should be meticulously planned, briefed, and "chair flown" by all crewmembers. There should be no doubt as to the sequence, limitations, preconditions, and "knock it off" criteria. If necessary, fly the entire test card in the simulator with all three crew. (If the profile gets this deep, however, consider calling in a production flight test crew from the manufacturer.)

- Have it in writing. The profile from preflight to debrief should be well planned and the specific sequence and conditions written down. Each test should have its own test card (not longer than one page) that has each step, restrictions, conditions, notes, cautions, warnings and required data to be recorded explicitly spelled out. "Knock it off" criteria must be spelled out for each test.

Going Forward

E-4B Sunset (55 SRW/PA USAF Photo)

The Air Force decided it had too many pilots so it gave majors with no chance of promotion a pat on the back and a kick in the pants out the door. For many the boot came with a severance check of $17,000 for 15 years of service to their country and nothing more. Those majors who were promoted but didn't garner school selections were allowed to either stay or separate with fat bonus checks and all prior committments waived.

For those of us with school assignments that was pretty much the only option available. We could separate from the Air Force but would get no bonus, no severance, and no pat on the back.

Within six months the squadron was without any majors, but that wasn't my problem. I found myself in Montgomery, Alabama with nearly six hundred highly qualified officers from various countries and military services, led by a cadre of officers of a somewhat lower standard. After one week it became obvious that the instructional material was put together in a haphazard fashion, making it unsuitable for learning.

"This is garbage," I said to the *Lovely Mrs. Haskel* in a fit of frustration. "They've simply cobbled together two hundred pages of disjointed readings for us every night and expect us to learn. How can you learn when the instructors are so lazy?"

"Was it any different in your last two squadrons?" she asked. "What would you do if this was a flying squadron?"

"I would write my own textbooks," I said. She looked at me, in her wordless way that spoke volumes. So for the next year, every night, I wrote lessons.

Each day ended with an assignment to read between 100 and 200 pages of material, most of it poorly written. But skimming the entire assignment first made it easy to pick the wheat from the chaff and the entire exercise rarely took more than three or four hours. I was acing the exams, the speeches, and all the written papers.

One part of our duties was to instruct our fellow students once a week so the read / write / instruct process became intuitive after a while. In an unmilitary act of altruism, I started photocopying each lesson's notes for a few friends. After a few weeks an underground network evolved that managed to furnish all 600 students with a copy of the notes before 9 a.m. every morning.

After a few months, it became obvious to the faculty that some students were forgoing the readings completely in favor of these notes. But they preferred having their students actually pass the exams than complain to me. I knew I had the program wired and thought I was going to escape the year without distinction or penalty. I was wrong.

One week before graduation the commandant of the school asked to see me and announced I had earned "top grad" honors.

"How is that possible?" I asked. "I certainly didn't ace the program."

"No," he said, "you did not. But you came awfully close. Besides, your notes got most of the class through and we've never had a higher graduation rate. You must have been one helluva instructor pilot. Judging by your test scores you knew all this stuff already. How a pilot knows so much about geopolitics is beyond me."

"Truth is I didn't," I said. "But I seem to learn best when I am teaching others. So when you get right down to it, handing out my notes was just a way of motivating myself to keep the notes at a high standard. It was a selfish act, in the end."

"Selfish or not," he said, "being a top grad out of six hundred has to count for something. I can guarantee you any assignment. I have the top offices in the Pentagon willing to take you. And if you want an overseas assignment, there are more than a few staff jobs out there who will be thrilled to have you. Major, you name your assignment."

It was a tempting offer. There were a lot of crummy staff jobs out there but there were some really good ones too. I hadn't touched an airplane for a year and somehow survived. Was I really ready to quit?

"Any job, general?" I asked.

"You name it, son."

"General, I am an instructor at heart. No, more than that. I am a flight instructor at heart. I heard the 89th at Andrews has brand new Gulfstreams. Sir, I know this isn't what the Air Force wants. But it is what I want."

He looked at me in disbelief. He wore command pilot wings and I knew from his bio he spent five years at the Hanoi Hilton after being shot down in his F-105. He hadn't flown or walked without a limp ever since. I meant no disrespect. I realized that thought was completely immaterial. Was disrespect sensed?

"Helluva a loss for the Pentagon," he said. "But you got it. I hope you don't regret this ten years from now."

"Me too, sir," I said. "But at heart, I am an instructor pilot."

As I left his office, my return to the cockpit guaranteed, a voice from my past came to me.

"So grasshopper, the student becomes the master. Excellent."

References

14 CFR 21, Title 14: Aeronautics and Space, Certification Procedures for Products and Parts, Federal Aviation Administration, Department of Transportation

14 CFR 25, Title 14: Aeronautics and Space, Airworthiness Standards: Transport Category Airplanes, Federal Aviation Administration, Department of Transportation

14 CFR 91, Title 14: Aeronautics and Space, General Operating and Flight Rules, Federal Aviation Administration, Department of Transportation

14 CFR 97, Title 14: Aeronautics and Space, Standard Instrument Procedures, Federal Aviation Administration, Department of Transportation

14 CFR 121, Title 14: Aeronautics and Space, Operating Requirements: Domestic, Flag, and Supplemental Operations, Federal Aviation Administration, Department of Transportation

Advisory Circular 61-107B, Aircraft Operations at Altitudes Above 25,000 Feet Mean Sea Level or Mach Numbers Greater than .75, 3/29/13, U.S. Department of Transportation

Advisory Circular 120-80A, In-flight Fires, 12/22/14, U.S. Department of Transportation

Aeronautical Information Manual, U.S. Department of Transportation

Air Force Manual (AFM) 51-37, Instrument Flying, 1 December 1976

Air Training Command Manual (ATCM) 51-3, Aerodynamics for Pilots, 15 November 1963

Casadevall, Thomas J., Advances in Volcanic Ash Avoidance and Recovery, Boeing Commercial Airplanes Group, U.S. Geological Survey, undated

Cortés, Antonio, CRM Leadership & Followership 2.0, ERAU Department of Aeronautical Science, 2008

Crew Resource Management: An Introductory Handbook, DOT/FAA/RD-92/26, DOT-VNTSC-FAA-92-8, Research and Development Service, Washington, DC, August 1992

Hurt, H. H., Jr., Aerodynamics for Naval Aviators, NAVWEPS 00-80T-80, Skyhorse Publishing, Inc., New York NY, 2012

ICAO Annex 14 - Aerodromes - Vol I - Aerodrome Construction and Design, International Standards and Recommended Practices, Annex 14 to the Convention on International Civil Aviation, Vol I, July 2009

ICAO Doc 8168 - Aircraft Operations - Vol I - Flight Procedures, Procedures for Air Navigation Services, International Civil Aviation Organization, 2006

ICAO Doc 9974 - Flight Safety and Volcanic Ash, 2012

ICAO Doc 9691 - Manual on Volcanic Ash, Radioactive Material and Toxic Chemical Clouds, 2001.

Kanki, Barbara; Helmreich, Robert; and Anca, José, Crew Resource Management, Academic Press, Amsterdam, 2010

Shein, Karsten, Cinder and Ash Hazards, Professional Pilot, August 2013, pp. 86 - 90

Technical Order 1-1-300, Maintenance Operational Checks and Check Flights, Secretary of the Air Force, 15 March 2012

Technical Order 1C-135(K)A-1, Flight Handbook, Secretary of the Air Force, 25 April 1957

United States Standard for Terminal Instrument Procedures (TERPS), Federal Aviation Administration 8260.3B CHG 25, 03/09/2012

Index of Flight Lessons

About the Author

James Albright is an average pilot with average stick and rudder skills, but has an above average desire to learn and instruct. He spent twenty years in the United States Air Force as an aircraft commander, instructor pilot, evaluator pilot, and squadron commander. After retiring as a lieutenant colonel, he went on to fly for several private and commercial operators as an international captain, check airman, and chief pilot. His logbook includes the T-37B, T-38A, KC-135A, Boeing 707, Boeing 747, Challenger 604, and the Gulfstream III, IV, V, and 450.

His website, www.code7700.com attracts a million hits each month and his articles have appeared in several magazines, most notably Business & Commercial Aviation.

While he claims to be devoid of ego, that can hardly be true of someone willing to write a five volume set of flight lessons based on his own experiences.

CPSIA information can be obtained
at www.ICGtesting.com
Printed in the USA
BVOW11s1051150317
478564BV00011B/322/P